yOung
Exceptional
children

DEC

Monograph Series No. 8

Supporting Social Emotional
Development in Young Children

THE DIVISION FOR EARLY CHILDHOOD
OF THE COUNCIL FOR EXCEPTIONAL CHILDREN

D1362089

Eva M. Horn an

Co-Editors

Disclaimer

The opinions and information contained in the articles in this publication are those of the authors of the respective articles and not necessarily those of the co-editors of the *Young Exceptional Children (YEC)* Monograph Series or of the Division for Early Childhood. Accordingly, the Division of Early Childhood assumes no liability or risk that may be incurred as a consequence, directly or indirectly, of the use and application of any of the contents of this publication.

The DEC does not perform due diligence on advertisers, exhibitors, or their products or services, and cannot endorse or guarantee that their offerings are suitable or accurate.

27 Fort Missoula Road, Suite 2
Missoula, MT 59804
(406) 543-0872 • FAX (406) 543-0887
www.dec-sped.org

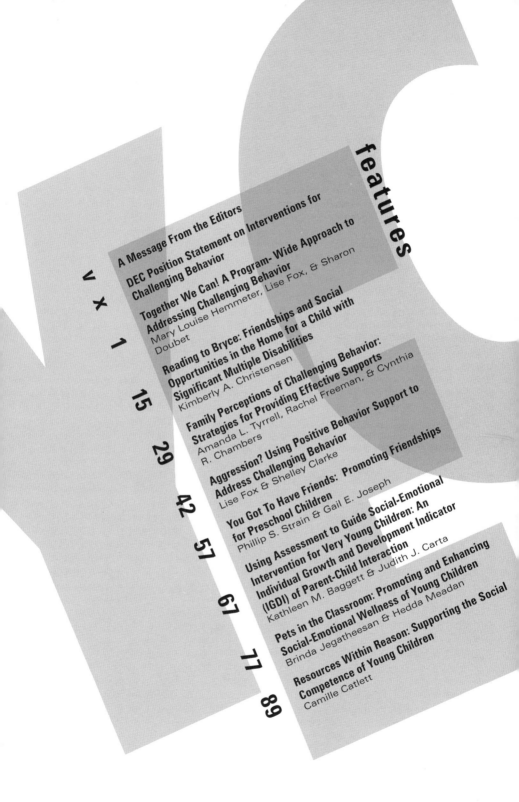

features

A Message From the Editors

Welcome to the eighth issue of the Young Exceptional Children Monograph Series. In this issue, we address the topic of infant, toddler, and young children's social-emotional development.

Given the current emphasis on academic achievement, it is critical that young children's social-emotional development not be overlooked, especially since considerable research indicates that success in school is strongly linked to early positive social-emotional development. The content of this monograph extends that of the first YEC monograph, Practical Ideas for Addressing Challenging Behavior, by including articles that address a range of issues related to social-emotional development. As always, each of the articles in this monograph highlights practices found in DEC Recommended Practices in Early Intervention/Early Childhood Special Education (Sandall, Hemmeter, Smith, & McLean, 2005). The collection of articles in this monograph addresses the values, beliefs, and practices inherent in the recommended practices. They do so by describing specific strategies that will assist practitioners, together in partnership with families, to support and enhance the social-emotional development of infants, toddlers, and young children with special needs in their care. In addition, we provide a reprint of DEC's position paper on interventions for challenging behaviors. You are encouraged to copy this statement and share it with your colleagues.

The first article by Hemmeter and colleagues lays a strong foundation for the importance of a program-wide approach to addressing challenging behaviors. A three-tiered (i.e., universal, secondary, and tertiary strategies) school-wide positive behavior support (PBS) model has been developed and implemented by our professional colleagues working with school-aged students to address the behavior support needs of all students in a school. Hemmeter and her colleagues describe a framework developed for early childhood programs that reflects the three-tiered model of program-wide positive behavior support and then provide the reader with specific guidelines for the process of implementing such a model in an early childhood program.

However, innovations are not always initiated by larger systems, but rather by an individual or group of individuals closest to the child. Reading to Bryce is one family's story of how they created opportunities for their son with significant multiple disabilities to interact with other children. Christensen describes the nine steps this family used to develop a volunteer program of reading to Bryce. This story is an excellent example of how the collaborative efforts of a family, school, and community can have exciting results for a young boy, his family, and peers.

The third article by Tyrrell, Freeman, and Chambers reminds us to pause and remember to take the perspective of the other members of our team—in this case, the perspective of the family as we plan and work to support young children's emotional development. Given that challenging behavior has an impact on children as well as families, understanding challenging behavior in the context of families is critical. Tyrrell and her colleagues describe the impact of children's challenging behavior on families, discuss supports that families have identified as beneficial, and provide examples of strategies that professionals can use to more effectively work together in partnership with families.

Fox and Clarke continue the theme of reminding us of the importance of working together in collaborative teams with thoughtful planning to guide our development, implementation, and continued assessment of the success of our interventions. They provide us with a comprehensive description of the use of PBS by early educators to develop and implement effective behavior support plans specifically focused on young children who engage in aggressive behaviors. Through the story of Cooper they illustrate how the process works and the outcomes that may be experienced.

Up to this point, each of the articles has addressed information on intervention and interaction strategies that adults can do to support children's positive social behaviors and prevent the display of challenging behaviors. The next article by Strain and Joseph turns our attention to the importance of friendships in the lives of young children and their healthy social-emotional development. It has been well documented that many children with special needs do not develop friendship skills without thoughtful, well-planned instruction. The authors provide valuable information on the fundamental importance of friendship skills along with a straightforward set of strategies to support children in learning the specific skills that have been documented as most likely to lead to friendships. They are, as stated by the authors, "strategies to maximize children's opportunities to live in a social world where everyone knows their name."

Assessment for monitoring progress is a crucial component of all early childhood special education programs. In their article, Baggett and Carta discuss the Indicator of Parent-Child Interaction (IPCI), an example of an Individual Growth and Development Indicator. The IPCI is described as a means of checking growth toward the general outcome of interactions between a parent or caregiver and his or her child. This measure provides the early interventionist a means to assess, develop appropriate intervention, and monitor that intervention for growth in social-emotional competence.

Finally, Jegatheesan and Meadan share with us the many contributions animals can make in children's lives, especially related to their social and emotional development. This article helps us to understand the influence pets in the classroom can have and provides guidelines for teachers to introduce pets to children. They further illustrate activities with pets that can help teachers facilitate children's social interactions and help these children develop self-esteem, self-awareness, a sense of compassion, and empathy.

This eighth monograph ends, as have the previous editions, with Camille Catlett's "Resources Within Reason," Just as with each issue of *Young Exceptional Children*, Camille has provided you with low-cost but high-quality resources for materials to support your efforts in facilitating the healthy social-emotional development of the young children in your care.

As you read the articles in this monograph, we hope that you are inspired to reflect upon your practices with infants, toddlers, and young children with special needs, and their families, and that families find support for their search for responsive services. Change in our behaviors should lead us toward our goal of families and professionals practicing shared responsibility and collaboration to support the healthy social-emotional development of all young children.

Contributing Reviewers

Rashida Banerjee, University of Kansas
Ann Bingham, University of Nevada-Reno
Patty Blasco, Oregon Health Sciences University
Joanna Burton, University of Illinois at Urbana-Champaign
Virginia Buysse, University of North Carolina at Chapel Hill
Nitasha Clark, Vanderbilt University
Lynette Chandler, Northern Illinois University
Lise Fox, University of South Florida
Misty Goosen, University of Kansas
Jennifer Grisham-Brown, University of Kentucky
Sarah Hadden, University of Virginia
Mary Louise Hemmeter, Vanderbilt University
Cheryl Hitchcock, Tennessee Technological University
Lee Ann Jung, University of Kentucky
Jean Kang, University of Kansas
Gwiok Kim, University of Kansas
Cecile Komara, University of Alabama
Angela Lee, University of Illinois at Urbana-Champaign
Dave Lindeman, University of Kansas
Mary McLean, University of Wisconsin-Milwaukee
Marisa Macy, University of Oregon
Kristen Missal, University of Kentucky
Linda Mitchell, Wichita State University
Andrea Morris, Southern Illinois University Carbondale
Missy Olive, University of Texas
Susan Palmer, University of Kansas
Yanhui Pang, Tennessee Technological University
Carla Peterson, Iowa State University
Diane Plunkett, University of Kansas
Kristi Pretti-Frontczak, Kent State University

Paige Pullen, University of Virginia
Cathy Qi, University of New Mexico
Beth Rous, University of Kentucky
Rosa Milgaros Santos, University of Illinois at Urbana-Champaign
Ilene Schwartz, University of Washington
Tamara Sewell, Tennessee Technological University
Shelia Smith, University of Kansas
Dawn Thomas, University of Illinois at Urbana-Champaign
Vickie Turbiville, Dripping Springs, TX
Amanda Tyrrell, University of Kansas
Robin Wells, Eastern New Mexico University
Mike Wischnowski, St. John Fischer College
Barbara Wolfe, University of St. Thomas

Reference

Sandall, S., Hemmeter, M. L., Smith, B. S., & McLean, M. (2005). *DEC recommended practices: A comprehensive guide*. Longmont, CO: Sopris West.

Co-Editors: Eva Horn   Hazel Jones
                    evahorn@ku.edu   HAjones@coe.ufl.edu

Coming Next!

The topic for the eighth *YEC* Monograph is "Linking Curriculum to Child and Family Outcomes." For more information, check the "Announcements" section of *Young Exceptional Children* (Volume 10, Number 1) or go to **http:/www.dec-sped.org.**

Position Statement on Interventions for Challenging Behavior

Adopted: April 1998
Reaffirmed: June 2001

Many young children engage in challenging behavior in the course of early development. The majority of these children respond to developmentally appropriate management techniques.

Every parent, including parents of young children with disabilities, wants his or her child to attend schools, child-care centers, or community-based programs that are nurturing and safe. Many young children engage in challenging behavior at various times during their early development. Typically, this behavior is short-term and decreases with age and use of appropriate guidance strategies. However, for some children these incidences of challenging behavior may become more consistent despite increased adult vigilance and use of appropriate guidance strategies. For these children, the challenging behavior may result in injury to themselves or others, cause damage to the physical environment, interfere with the acquisition of new skills, and/or socially isolate the child (Doss & Reichle, 1991). Additional intervention efforts may be required for these children.

DEC believes strongly that many types of services and intervention strategies are available to address challenging behavior.

Given the developmental nature of most challenging behavior, we believe that there is a vast array of supplemental services that can be added to the home and education environment to increase the likelihood that children will learn appropriate behavior. A variety of intervention strategies can be implemented with either formal or informal support. Services and strategies could include, but are not limited to: (a) designing environments and activities to prevent challenging behavior and to help all children develop appropriate behavior; (b) utilizing effective behavioral interventions that are positive and address both form and function of a young child's challenging behavior; (c) adopting curricular modification and accommodation strategies designed to help young children learn behaviors appropriate to their settings; and (d) providing external consultation and technical assistance or additional staff support. In addition, all professionals who work with children in implementing IEPs or IFSPs must have opportunities to acquire knowledge and skills necessary for effective implementation of prevention and intervention programs.

DEC believes strongly that families play a critical role in designing and carrying out effective interventions for challenging behavior.

Given the family-focused nature of early childhood education, we acknowledge the critical role that families play in addressing challenging behavior. Often times, challenging behavior occurs across places, people and time, thus families are critical members of the intervention team. A coordinated effort between family members and professionals is needed to assure that interventions are effective and efficient and address both child and family needs and strengths.

All decisions regarding the identification of a challenging behavior, possible interventions, placement, and ongoing evaluation must be made in accordance with the family through the IEP, IFSP, or other team decision-making processes.

Reference
Doss, L.S. & Reichle, J.(1991). Replacing excess behavior with an initial communicative repertoire. In J. Reichle, J. York, & J. Sigafoos (Eds.), *Implementing augmentative and alternative communication: Strategies for learners with serve disabilities*. Baltimore: Brooks Publishing Co.

This DEC position endorsed by the following organizations:

Division for Early Childhood
27 Fort Missoula Road, Suite 2
Missoula, Montana 59804
Phone: (406)543-0872
Fax: (406) 543-0887
Email: dec@dec-sped.org
www.dec-sped.org

Together We Can! A Program-Wide Approach to Addressing Challenging Behavior

Mary Louise Hemmeter, Ph.D.,
Vanderbilt University

Lise Fox, Ph.D.,
University of South Florida

Sharon Doubet, M.S.Ed.,
University of Illinois at Urbana Champaign

We do training on challenging behavior every year, and it is still a big problem for our program! (An administrator)

I get so frustrated with dealing with challenging behavior. Sometimes I want to quit! (An early childhood teacher)

I can deal with the everyday behavior problems, but I just don't know what to do with Jeremy, whose aggressive behavior is disrupting my class every single day and is dangerous to the other children in the classroom. (An early childhood teacher)

Young children's challenging behavior is a significant issue in many early childhood programs. Teachers report increasing numbers of children with challenging behavior and increasing frustration associated with dealing with challenging behavior (Hemmeter, Corso, & Cheatham, 2006). Recent studies of preschool children have found rates of reported problem behavior ranging from 9%–33% depending on the population of children being studied (Campbell, 1995; Qi & Kaiser, 2003). Children with early-appearing externalizing behaviors (e.g., tantrums, aggression toward others or self) are at-risk for both social and academic problems, including limited access to instruction and peer and teacher rejection (LaRocque, Brown, & Johnson, 2001). Without appropriate intervention during the preschool years, these children enter school at-risk for social, emotional, behavioral, and academic problems.

When children with challenging behavior do not have access to effective interventions early, the stability of problem behavior over time is well established (Campbell, 1995; Shaw, Gilliom, & Giovannelli, 2000). However, there is evidence that the interventions and supports needed during the preschool years are often not available in early childhood settings. Studies have documented the relatively low quality of group care settings and have linked the quality of those settings to poorer child outcomes related to social-emotional development (Helburn et al., 1995; National Research Council, 2001; NICHD, 1999). High-quality, developmentally appropriate environments are a critical feature of effective approaches for addressing the needs of children with challenging behavior. Further evidence for the lack of support in early childhood programs comes from a study that children in state-funded prekindergarten programs were six times more likely to be expelled from preschool then children in K-12 (Gilliam, 2005). While this rate was cut in half when the teacher had access to behavioral consultation, a majority of the teachers reported not having access to these consultants. In addition, studies have identified challenging behavior as a primary training need of early childhood educators (Buscemi, Bennett, Thomas, & Deluca, 1995; Hemmeter et al., 2006). This indicates that early childhood educators in many cases do not feel prepared to deal effectively with challenging behaviors. These findings taken together suggest that the quality and expertise needed to address the behavioral and social-emotional needs of children is often missing in early childhood programs. In order to build the capacity of programs to meet the needs of children with challenging behavior, an approach is needed that includes not only training for teachers, but also access to behavior support expertise and the provision of support from administrators and program policies.

Positive Behavior Support (PBS) was developed about 20 years ago in response to the use of aversive intervention procedures to address the challenging behavior of individuals with developmental disabilities and severe problem behavior. In the last decade, the application of the tenets and practices of PBS to the entire school population within elementary, middle, and high schools has evolved (Horner, Sugai, Todd, & Lewis-Palmer, 2005). School-wide PBS was developed as a strategy for approaching behavior from a systems perspective, in which systems and procedures are established within schools to support the promotion of children's appropriate behaviors as well as to address the needs of children with more significant behavioral issues (Freeman et al., 2006; Sugai, Sprague, Horner, & Walker, 2000).

The school-wide PBS model uses a three-tiered approach of universal, secondary, and tertiary strategies to address the behavior support needs

Figure 1
The Teaching Pyramid Model (adapted from Fox, et al., 2003 with permission)

Tertiary — Individualized Interventions

Secondary — **Social-Emotional Learning Strategies**

Universal — **Prevention Practices in Home and Classroom Settings**

Building Positive Relationships with Children and Families

of all students in a school. Universal strategies are focused on the development of a school culture where behavior expectations are explicitly taught and promoted by all school staff. Secondary strategies are used to address the needs of students who are at-risk of developing more serious problem behavior. Finally, tertiary strategies are focused on developing individualized support for students who have persistent and severe challenging behavior (Freeman et al., 2006). The adoption of school-wide PBS has resulted in decreases in problem behavior, decreases in in-school and out-of-school suspensions, and increases in instructional time (Horner et al., 2005; Nelson, Martella, & Marchand-Martell, 2002). While the school-wide PBS model is well established, relatively little work has been done on applications of this approach in early childhood settings.

There are a number of characteristics of early childhood programs that potentially affect the translation of the school-wide PBS model for adoption within early education settings. These characteristics include the variety of service delivery systems that are involved in providing services to young children (e.g., Head Start, Public Schools, Child Care), the philosophical approaches used in early childhood settings, the age and abilities of young children, the training of teachers, and access to behavior support expertise. The purpose of this article is to describe how school-wide PBS may be applied in a manner that addresses the unique needs of early childhood programs and the young children participating in the programs. This article will describe a framework developed for early childhood programs that reflects the three-tiered model of universal, secondary, and tertiary strategies and the implementation process for program-wide adoption of that model (i.e., program-wide PBS).

Program-Wide PBS: Adopting the Teaching Pyramid

The *Teaching Pyramid* (Fox, Dunlap, Hemmeter, Joseph, & Strain, 2003) provides guidance for how to promote young children's social-emotional development and address challenging behavior. The *Teaching Pyramid* (Figure 1) includes universal promotion practices at two levels, secondary intervention practices for children at-risk, and tertiary interventions for children with persistent challenging behavior. The *Teaching Pyramid* is based on research on effective instruction for young children (National Research Council, 2001), promotion of children's social competence (Guralnick & Neville, 1997; Webster-Stratton, 1999; Hyson, 2004), and positive behavior support (Fox, Dunlap, & Cushing, 2002; Fox, Dunlap, & Powell, 2002).

As illustrated in Figure 1, the four levels of practices in the *Teaching Pyramid* are positive relationships, supportive environments, social-emotional teaching strategies, and individualized interventions. *Positive relationships* with children, families, and colleagues provide a context for supporting children's social-emotional development and addressing challenging behavior. *Supportive environments* refer to practices such as positive attention, consistent routines, clear expectations and well-designed physical spaces that promote children's engagement and success in the classroom (Strain & Hemmeter, 1999; Lawry, Danko, & Strain, 1999). Social-emotional teaching strategies are necessary to address the social, communicative, and emotional delays that often lead to challenging behavior (Webster-Stratton, 1999; Joseph & Strain, 2003). *Individualized interventions* will be needed because even when the first three levels of the *Teaching Pyramid* are in place, a small number of children are likely to continue to engage in challenging behavior. These children will need an individualized behavior support plan that is based on an understanding of their challenging behavior (Fox et al., 2002).

Strategies for Program-Wide Implementation of the Teaching Pyramid

Program-wide adoption of the *Teaching Pyramid* (i.e., program-wide PBS) includes a number of steps that are described in the following pages and summarized in Table 1. We provide an illustration of each step by describing the program-wide PBS implementation efforts of the

Table 1
Steps to Implementing a Program-Wide Model

1. Establish a leadership team and develop goals for the plan

2. Develop a plan for program-wide adoption
   a. Develop a plan for involving families
   b. Develop a plan for getting staff buy-in
   c. Develop program-wide expectations
   d. Develop strategies for teaching and acknowledging the expectations
   e. Develop a process for addressing ongoing problem behavior

3. Develop a professional development plan

4. Develop and implement a plan for monitoring outcomes

Valeska Hinton Early Childhood Education Center (VHECEC). VHECEC is a NAEYC-accredited, public school program that serves 400 children in preschool through first grade. This center includes public school, Special Education, Head Start, State Block Grant Programs (Pre-K At-Risk, Family Education), Title I, Early Head Start, Even Start, and GED programs. As they were developing their program-wide initiative, they selected the slogan "Together We Can" to refer to their approach.

Establish a Program-Wide PBS Leadership Team and Develop Goals

Program-wide PBS begins with establishing a leadership team that includes staff and administrators, families, and other professionals who might provide support to the program around children's challenging behavior or mental health. The team should include an administrator who has the authority to make decisions about policies and procedures, curriculum changes, and professional development activities. Programs should include staff who are not directly involved in classrooms but who interact with children on a regular basis, such as bus drivers, custodians, or cooks. One of the first tasks for the leadership team is to establish goals for program-wide PBS based on data on the needs of the children and staff in their program.

VHECEC administrators discussed the growing need to support children, teachers and families in the areas of social and emotional skill development and challenging behavior. Their staff survey revealed the most-requested training need was how to address challenging behaviors. When children exhibited persistent challenging behaviors, staff members often felt unsupported, frustrated, and overwhelmed.

Table 2

Taking it Home: Ideas for Promoting Family Involvement Related to Program-Wide Behavior Support

- Introduce the adoption of the behavior support plan in a family newsletter
- Host an event where the plan is described and children demonstrate the expectations
- Provide families with tips for teaching the expectations at home
- Send home "Look at Me" notes that provide a photo of the child engaging in the expectation
- Provide families with lists of children's books on topics related to social-emotional development
- Provide families with ways to promote social-emotional development at home
- Provide families with "homework" assignments to practice social skills that are fun for the family to do with their child (e.g., "give each person in your family 3 compliments" or "ask each family member to identify a best friend and what they like about that person")
- Host program celebrations of success and invite family members to attend
- Display the expectations in the entryway of your center including pictures of children and staff demonstrating the expectations and child generated dictations of examples of the expectations
- Develop an overview of the process that will be used to develop behavior support plans for children. Include a list of frequently asked questions, a description of what behavior support means, how families will be involved, and quotes from families who have previously been involved. Share this with all families at an initial parent conference

The administrative team wanted to develop a plan for addressing social and emotional development and challenging behavior that would focus on the following goals: increasing time for instruction, helping staff feel supported, providing staff with effective strategies, and involving parents. After investigating a variety of approaches, they found that the Teaching Pyramid represented an approach that was consistent with their program philosophy and included all the criteria they were looking for, including instruction and promotion of positive social behavior, prevention of challenging behavior, and the provision of individual supports for children with persistent challenging behavior.

A Leadership Team was established by asking staff to sign up if they were interested in being on the team. The staff that volunteered to serve on the team included teachers, classroom assistants, family services workers, after school care providers, administrators, and other non-classroom staff. The team was facilitated by the Professional Development Coordinator.

Develop a Program-Wide PBS Implementation Plan

The first major task for the Leadership Team is to develop a program-wide implementation plan. The plan should address: (1) the involvement of families in all phases of the initiative; (2) staff buy in for the plan; (3) identification of program-wide expectations for children's behavior; (4) strategies for teaching and acknowledging the expectations; and (5) a process for developing individualized behavior support plans for children with ongoing challenging behavior.

Develop a Plan for Involving Families. Families should be involved in the development, implementation, and evaluation of the plan. Families can serve on the Leadership Team, or the Leadership Team can meet with families on a regular basis to get their input into the plan. It will be important for the team to hear from families about their concerns about children's behavior, the types of information they would like to receive, how they would like to be involved in addressing children's challenging behavior, and the format and strategies that would be most useful for sharing information with families. Ideas for involving families are included in Table 2.

At Valeska Hinton, families were kept informed and invited to participate in the development of the program-wide PBS implementation plan. Monthly parent meetings included updates about the process and encouraged input and feedback. The program's existing Parent Leadership Team was asked to participate in meetings to provide input and feedback into the plan. The school's ongoing structures for involving families (e.g., parent teacher conferences, home visits, informal interactions at drop off and pickup) were used as opportunities for sharing information with families about social-emotional development, strategies for supporting children's behavior, and the program-wide plan. For example, one set of parent-teacher conferences was used for sharing with the families the program wide expectations and how they could be supported at home. Parent workshops to introduce the plan were planned.

Develop a Plan for Getting Staff Buy-In. It will be important to have buy-in from the majority of staff prior to implementing program-wide PBS. The success of a program-wide approach will be in part dependent on the extent to which the plan is implemented consistently across all staff. There are several ways to establish buy-in from staff including inviting them to serve on the planning team,

It will be important to have buy-in from the majority of staff prior to implementing program-wide PBS

Table 3
Together We Can! Behavior Expectations for Adults and Children in Our School

Expectation	Playground	Hall	Classroom	Bus
Be respectful	Take care of each other Take turns Take care of our playground	Use inside voices Stay together	Share Be fair Listen to others Care about others' feelings	Follow directions Stay in your own space Take care of the bus
Be safe	Follow playground rules Play safely Play where you can see your teacher	Use helping hands and walking feet Stay with your teacher Make sure the teacher knows where you are	Use walking feet Play safely Follow directions Keep our room clean	Stay with your teachers Stay seated When buses are moving – stop, look, and listen Ask a grown-up for help
Be a team player	Share outdoor toys Help park the bikes Work it out with words	Stay with the group Help each other	Share ideas Help each other Work it out with words	Help others Stay with the group

holding focus groups with small groups of staff to solicit their input and asking them to sign a letter of commitment. Most schools with successful program-wide initiatives require teachers to sign a letter of commitment or in some other way indicate their commitment to the initiative prior to the plan being implemented in the school.

While Valeska Hinton did not have staff sign a letter of commitment, they implemented several steps to ensure staff buy-in. They invited volunteers to serve on the planning committee. When 20 staff members volunteered, all of them were included on the planning team. As each step of the plan was developed, the team shared information with staff throughout the building and provided opportunities for discussion and feedback at ongoing staff meetings. At critical points during the planning, the team members individually talked with staff to get input or feedback.

Develop Program-Wide Expectations. A key step in the development of program-wide PBS will be the identification of expectations for children's behavior. Behavior expectations serve two important purposes: providing staff, children, and families with a common language built around supporting children's social skills and appropriate behaviors, and providing a consistent message to children about their behavior. This shifts the focus from challenging behavior to supporting children's appropriate behavior and social skills. Further, by having all adults focused on common expectations for children's behavior, it increases the frequency with which children receive consistent input and positive feedback about their behavior. Table 3 provides a sample matrix of how expectations can be addressed across settings within the school.

Behavior expectations serve two important purposes: providing staff, children, and families with a common language built around supporting children's social skills and appropriate behaviors, and providing a consistent message to children about their behavior.

After many hours of engaging debates, the VHECEC planning team came to consensus on the program-wide behavior expectations: "Children and adults at VHECEC are expected to be respectful, be safe, and be team players." An important lesson learned through this process was the need to establish expectations not just for children's behavior but also for adults' behavior. Thus, these expectations reflect a commitment to holding staff accountable for demonstrating these same behaviors in their interactions with children, colleagues, and families.

Develop Strategies for Teaching and Acknowledging the Expectations. Once the expectations have been developed, the team develops a process for teaching and acknowledging the expectations. This process involves developing a timeline for teaching the expectations across settings within the school, strategies for teaching the expectations, and strategies for acknowledging the expectations in individual classrooms as well as program-wide. A program-wide plan for teaching and acknowledging the expectations helps to ensure that children are learning and being supported in their use of the expectations across all the settings and adults with whom they interact each day. The expectations can be taught using a variety of teaching strategies, including discussion, role play, modeling, and feedback in context. The expectations can be acknowledged informally through positive feedback from adults and more formally through bulletin boards, photographs, and recognition in public areas of the school.

The Together We Can team developed a list of strategies for teaching the expectations and a plan for how the whole school could focus on one expectation at the same time, integrating the expectations into their use of their social skills curriculum, modeling and role- playing expectations, photos of students demonstrating the expectations, and many more ways. Acknowledgement strategies were developed to recognize prosocial behavior. These strategies included verbal descriptive feedback, photos of the children engaged in an expectation displayed on a bulletin board in the center court of the building, and a book developed by a class that included pictures and descriptions of children engaging in the expectations.

Develop a Process for Addressing Ongoing Problem Behavior. While the above promotion and prevention activities are effective for meeting the social and emotional needs of most children, some children will need individualized intervention plans. The program-wide plan will include the development of a process for addressing the needs of those children with persistent behavior. A staff person is identified who has the responsibility of facilitating this process with teams around individual children.

During the second year of Together We Can, team members focused on the development of a plan for supporting children with the most significant problem behaviors. A process was developed for addressing the needs of children whose behavior was dangerous, disruptive, and persistent. Staff members were identified as behavior support facilitators and were trained in conducting observations, gathering information, and writing a behavior support plan for a child.

Design a Professional Development Plan

In order to implement program-wide PBS, a plan should be developed for training and supporting the staff on the model. Professional development for program staff should include an overview training that provides general information on the *Teaching Pyramid* and the processes that have been developed for supporting children with challenging behaviors. In addition, individualized and ongoing support should be planned for classroom teams based on their skills and needs related to addressing challenging behavior. These supports should include coaching in the classroom. Staff also should be trained in how to complete observations and participate in the development of individualized plans for children. Provisions should be made for training, orienting, and supporting new staff. Finally, plans should be made for how teachers and other staff will be recognized for their work related to supporting children's behavior.

As part of the Together We Can plan, several professional develop-ment activities were implemented. A series of inservice activities for all staff members were conducted on each level of the Teaching Pyramid (Fox et al., 2003). Administrators made plans for how they would orient new staff to the model. The professional development coordinator and lead teacher made themselves available to support teachers in their classrooms as the teachers implemented these strat-egies. Specific staff were identified and trained in how to facilitate the development of behavior support plans for individual children.

Develop a Plan for Monitoring Implementation and Outcomes of the Plan

The development of a program-wide PBS plan should be based on data on the needs of the children and staff in the program. These needs can be translated into goals or outcomes for the program-wide plan. It will be important to develop a plan for monitoring both the implementation and the outcomes of the plan. Regular data should be collected (e.g., incidences of problem behavior, requests from teachers for help around behavior) and used to revise the plan to ensure that important outcomes are being met.

Now that the plan components have been developed, the leadership meets to review the plan; arrange proactive education activities for staff, students, and families; advise the program's administrative team; and share updates at Staff Meetings. Outcomes of the PBS approach have included: program-wide agreement and focus on positive behavior support, an increased feeling of unity among staff members, shared language surrounding children's behaviors, and a reduction in children being "sent (taken) to the office".

Lessons Learned from Implementation of Program-Wide PBS

Program-wide PBS offers a systemic approach for addressing many of the key issues associated with challenging behavior in early childhood settings. Program-wide PBS not only provides a plan for training staff but also includes a focus on developing policies and procedures that are accessible and effective for supporting staff in addressing young children's social-emotional development and challenging behavior. It makes behavior support a "program-wide" issue and shifts the responsibility to the program rather than resting on the teacher. While program-wide PBS is a promising practice, it is difficult to implement. It is comprehensive and takes a long-term commitment. Based on our experiences with a variety of programs, we offer the following recommendations for implementing program-wide PBS in early childhood settings.

The first set of recommendations has to do with teaming and leadership. It is important to address issues related to school climate directly. Otherwise, it may affect the staff's ability to work together on this important project. Implement the plan using a team approach that is not dependent on any one staff member so that there is continued support when there are staff changes. Have a plan for orienting new staff, embedding questions about behavior support into interviews of potential staff, and supporting new staff in implementing the plan.

Ongoing training and support for staff over time is important. Dealing with challenging behaviors can be "challenging" for adults! Staff will need support in the form of training, consultation, problem solving, and acknowledgement. This support should be individualized, immediate, and effective. Remember to include all program staff in your plan. Bus drivers, cooks, custodians, related services staff, and administrators interact with children every day and are often faced with challenging behavior. Be sure that they too have the training and support to be effective in their interactions with children.

Include families from the beginning in all aspects of the planning and implementation. Families may need an orientation that includes a rationale for why this plan is needed in the first place. Make the PBS plan part of your parent handbook, parent orientation, home visit discussions, parent-teacher conferences, and other family activities. Post information about the plan and children's involvement in areas frequented by family members.

It is important to recognize the need for developing a plan that is both comprehensive and feasible. Avoid the temptation to focus on the few children in a program with the most problematic behaviors. Rather, focus on building a plan that promotes appropriate social skills and emotional competencies for all children, prevents challenging behavior, and finally, addresses challenging behaviors when they persist despite comprehensive promotion and prevention strategies. Finally, programs should realize that behavior support is an evolving and ongoing process.

In order to ensure that the plan is effective over time, a team will need to meet regularly to review program data and staff input, make changes in the plan as needed, and celebrate successes.

Note

You can reach Mary Louise Hemmeter by e-mail at ml.hemmeter@vanderbilt.edu

References

Buscemi, L., Bennett, T., Thomas, D., & Deluca, D.A. (1995). Head Start: Challenges and training needs. *Journal of Early Intervention, 20*(1), 1-13.

Campbell, S. B. (1995). Behavior problems in preschool children: A review of recent research. *Journal of Child Psychology and Psychiatry, 36*(1), 113-149.

Fox, L., Dunlap, G., & Cushing, L. (2002). Early intervention, positive behavior support, and transition to school. *Journal of Emotional and Behavior Disorders, 10*(3), 149-157.

Fox, L., Dunlap, G., Hemmeter, M.L., Joseph, G.E., & Strain, P.S. (2003). The teaching pyramid: A model for supporting social competence and preventing challenging behavior in young children. *Young Children, 58*, 48-52.

Fox, L., Dunlap, G., & Powell, D. (2002). Young children with challenging behavior: Issues and consideration for behavior support. *Journal of Positive Behavior Interventions, 4*, 208-217.

Freeman, R., Eber, L., Anderson, C., Irvin, L., Horner, R., Bounds, M., et al. (2006). Building inclusive school cultures using school-wide positive behavior support: Designing effective individual support systems for students with significant disabilities. *Research and Practice for Persons with Severe Disabilities, 31*, 4-17.

Gilliam, W. S. (2005). Prekindergarteners left behind: *Expulsion rates in state prekindergarten systems*. Retrieved July 20, 2005, from http://www.fcd-us.org/PDFs/NationalPreKExpulsionPaper03.02_new.pdf

Guralnick, M. J. & Neville, B. (1997). Designing early intervention programs to promote children's social competence. In M. J. Guralnick (Ed.), *The effectiveness of early intervention* (pp. 579-610). Baltimore: Paul H. Brookes.

Helburn, S., Culkin, M. I., Morris, J., Mocan, N., Howes, C., Phillipsen, L., et al. (1995). *Cost, quality, and child outcomes in child care centers*, public report, second edition. Denver: Economics Department, University of Colorado at Denver.

Hemmeter, M.L., Corso, R., & Cheatham, G. (2006, February). *Issues in addressing challenging behaviors in young children: A national survey of early childhood educators.* Paper presented at the Conference on Research Innovations in Early Intervention, San Diego, CA.

Horner, R. H., Sugai, G., Todd, A.W., & Lewis-Palmer, T. (2005). Schoolwide positive behavior support. In L. M. Bambara & L. Kern (Eds.), *Individualized supports for students with problem behaviors: Designing positive behavior plans* (pp. 359-390). New York: Guilford Press.

Hyson, M. (2004). *The emotional development of young children* (2nd ed.) New York: Teachers College Press.

Joseph, G. E. & Strain, P. S. (2003). Comprehensive evidence-based social-emotional curricula for young children: An analysis of efficacious adoption potential. *Topics in Early Childhood Special Education, 23*(2), 65-76.

LaRocque, M., Brown, S. E., & Johnson, K. L. (2001). Functional behavioral assessments and intervention plans in early intervention settings. *Infants and Young Children, 13*, 59-68.

Lawry, J., Danko, C., & Strain, P. (1999). Examining the role of the classroom environment in the prevention of problem behaviors. In S. Sandall & M. Ostrosky, (Eds.), *Young exceptional children: Practical ideas for addressing challenging behaviors* (pp. 49-62). Longmont, CO: Sopris West and Denver, CO: DEC.

National Research Council. (2001). *Eager to learn: Educating our preschoolers*. Committee on Early Childhood Pedagogy, Commission on Behavioral and Social Sciences and Education. B. T. Bowman, M. S. Donovan, & M. S. Burns (Eds.) Washington, DC: National Academy Press.

Nelson, J. R., Martella, R. M., & Marchand-Martella, N. M. (2002). Maximizing student learning: The effects of a comprehensive school-based program for preventing problem behaviors. *Journal of Emotional and Behavioral Disorders, 10*(3), 136-148.

NICHD Early Child Care Research Network. (1999, July). Child outcomes when child care center classes meet recommended standards for quality. *American Journal of Public Health, 89*(7), 1072-1077.

Qi, C. H. & Kaiser, A. P. (2003). Behavior problems of preschool children from low-income families: Review of the literature. *Topics in Early Childhood Special Education, 23*(4), 188-216.

Shaw, D., Gilliom, M., & Giovannelli, J. (2000). Aggressive behavior disorders. In C. H. Zeanah (Ed.), *Handbook of infant mental health* (pp. 397-411). New York: Guilford Press.

Sugai, G., Sprague, J. R., Horner, R. H., & Walker, H. M. (2000). Preventing school violence: The use of office discipline to assess a monitor school-wide discipline interventions. *Journal of Emotional and Behavioral Disorders, 8*(2), 94-101.

Strain, P. & Hemmeter, M. L. (1999). Keys to being successful. In S. Sandall & M. Ostrosky (Eds.), *Young exceptional children: Practical ideas for addressing challenging behaviors.* (pp. 17-28.) Longmont, CO: Sopris West and Denver, CO: DEC.

Webster-Stratton, C. (1999). *How to promote children's social and emotional competence.* London: Paul Chapman.

Reading to Bryce

Friendships and Social Opportunities in the Home for a Child with Significant Multiple Disabilities

Kimberly A. Christensen, M.Ed.
Bowling Green State University

Every day the children come to his home, alone or in pairs. Some are quiet and reserved, while others are giggly and animated. A few come carrying their own special books, but most select from shelves tightly packed with picture books, chapter books, and books that play music. They settle into a seat next to a little boy named Bryce and after warmly greeting him, begin to read. As the reader shares the story, Bryce grins and waves his arms to show his approval. The reader pauses and positions the book so Bryce can see the picture. Sometimes Bryce looks, while other times his eyes seem to be gazing far away. For thirty minutes, twice a day, this scene unfolds in Bryce's home, a timeless story of friends sharing a book together.

Children with and without disabilities need friends. Learning in young children often takes place within the contexts of social interactions. In addition to cognitive skill development, programs for young children should focus attention on social and emotional capabilities (National Scientific Council on the Developing Child, 2004). Opportunities to interact with peers in early care and education settings, as well as in the home and community are important contexts for children's development. Children with multiple disabilities must rely on significant adults to support peer relationships structuring the environment to promote engagement, social interaction, and communication. The DEC recommended practices suggest that teachers and parents do this by providing opportunities for children to be with their peers as well as for peers to serve as models, while the adults are responsive and imitative (Sandall, Hemmeter, Smith, & McLean, 2005). This article presents an innovative peer-reading volunteer program that promotes friendships and social opportunities in the home between a child with significant multiple dis-

Children with and without disabilities need friends.

abilities and children in his community. The vignettes that describe the program are in the words of the author, Bryce's mother.

Bryce is my son. He is medically fragile and has significant multiple disabilities as a result of a near-drowning accident at 18 months of age. The physicians told our family, after three months in the pediatric intensive care unit, that Bryce had poor rehabilitative potential. When he was discharged from the hospital, Bryce was functionally comatose and completely unresponsive. The doctors saved his life and now we had to give him a life worth living. Upon bringing Bryce home from the hospital at 22 months of age, our primary goal was to put a comprehensive program in place that would encourage him to become responsive to his environment and people around him by stimulating his vision, hearing, and touch. One component of this program has evolved beyond the original goal of eliciting responses to providing a structured opportunity for Bryce to have meaningful interactions with children in his home.

One component of this program has evolved beyond the original goal of eliciting responses to providing a structured opportunity for Bryce to have meaningful interactions with children in his home.

Rationale

A large body of research focuses on friendships and social opportunities for children with disabilities in school and other formal childhood settings (Bishop & Jubala, 1994; Evans, Salisbury, Palombaro, Berryman, & Hollowood, 1992; Guralnick, 1999; Hendrickson, Shokoohi-Yekta, Hamre-Nietupski, & Gable, 1996; Hollingsworth, 2005). Several programs and activities, such as *Circle of Friends* (Forest & Lusthaus, 1989), *Special Friends* (Cole, Vandercook, & Rynders, 1988), *The McGill Action Planning System* (MAPS) (described by Vandercook, York, & Forest, 1989), and *Creative Problem Solving* (Giangreco, Cloninger, Dennis, & Edelman, 2000) describe strategies to support the inclusion of students with disabilities in the school setting. While there are fewer studies investigating peer friendships and interactions in the home or neighborhood, researchers have found that children with severe cognitive disabilities tend to have limited social interactions in their homes with peers (Geisthardt, Brotherson, & Cook, 2002). Although parents want their children with disabilities to have opportunities for interactions with peers (Strully & Strully, 1985), Geisthardt and colleagues reported that many parents had resigned themselves to accept that their children would not have meaningful friendships. These researchers suggest that educators and administrators could have an important role in supporting parents to facilitate peer interactions. The effective use of students without disabilities as peer helpers is well documented (Hughes et al., 1999; Mastropieri & Scruggs, 2007; Staub & Hunt, 1993). Such programs are characterized by structured systematic approaches for training and supervising peers who voluntarily choose to interact with a child with disabilities. Supporting friendships in the home between children with significant disabilities and their peers in the community also requires an organized systematic approach.

A program to facilitate friendship and social opportunities in the home for a child with multiple disabilities requires parental involvement, structured social interactions, and support from educators and administrators. The remainder of this article describes the nine steps used to set up a peer-reading volunteer program, including strategies for support and supervision during the social interaction. These recommendations are based on the peer-reading model used in one child's home that spans ten years and involves over 150 peer readers.

A program to facilitate friendship and social opportunities in the home for a child with multiple disabilities requires parental involvement, structured social interactions, and support from educators and administrators.

Step One: Develop an Articulated Vision of Friendship for the Child

The first step is to develop an articulated vision of friendship for the child. This includes: (1) determining parental goals for the child's social interactions, (2) describing what social interactions could look like, and (3) discussing what would be necessary for the vision to become a reality. Research suggests that parents play a critical role in supporting social opportunities for their child with disabilities. Mainly parents who were successful in facilitating friendships for their son or daughter unconditionally accepted their child's disability and most often pursued social opportunities that included interaction with children who did not have disabilities (Turnbull, Pereira, and Blue-Banning, 1999).

Bryce was two years old when we proposed starting a reading volunteer program in our home. Our family had two goals in mind. Primarily, we hoped that hearing young children's voices on a regular basis might elicit a response in Bryce. A secondary motivation was

*our wish to increase his visibility in the community. Bryce's depen-
dence on medical technology and his fragile state of health limited
his experiences outside of the home. We felt that if Bryce could not
easily go out into the community and neighborhood, we would bring
the community and neighborhood to him. In the beginning, Bryce
was unresponsive to everything in his environment. He did not know
that the children were even at our home reading to him. However, we
wanted the children to know that Bryce was here, that he existed, and
that he was a member of their community.*

Step Two: Identify Existing Community Venues for Targeting Appropriate Peers

Many school systems and youth-oriented groups prioritize volunteerism
as an activity to address social responsibility and good citizenship, offering an infrastructure already in place to announce volunteer opportunities, schedule volunteer experiences, and provide administrative support.
Before contacting community venues, formulate a tentative proposal of
the volunteer program. Be flexible enough in the proposed idea to consider suggestions from the leadership of the community organization.

*We were aware of the strong initiative in our school system for pro-
moting volunteer service opportunities in school-age children. As a
result, our local school system had developed a volunteer program
headed by a retired school librarian, who worked part-time as the
volunteer coordinator. We called and presented the idea for a reading
volunteer program in our home for Bryce.*

Step Three: Determine the Structure of the Program

Research suggests that facilitating social interactions between children
with and without disabilities requires a structured approach (Downing,
2002; Salisbury, Gallucci, Palombaro, & Peck, 1995; Hollingsworth, 2005).
Promoting ongoing social opportunities in the home needs to be systematic and well organized as well. A reading volunteer program provides
such a structure by delineating a clear task for the peer participant.
Additionally, ongoing sustained interactions are supported by a program
design that enlists peer volunteers for a regular commitment. Components
to consider in the structure of the program include: (1) frequency of the
peer visits, (2) length of interactions, (3) age range of peers, (4) number
of peers present during the visit (e.g., one-on-one, pairs), and (5) location
of visits (e.g., in the home, in a community site).

The volunteer coordinator suggested we consider elementary students. She explained that they had fewer opportunities offered to them for volunteering. Also, because we lived in a neighborhood that was bordered by two elementary schools, children might be able to walk or bike to our house to read. We set up the program to have peers arrive nightly at 7:00 p.m. in our home to read for 30 minutes, either one-on-one with Bryce or in pairs. A letter was drafted and sent home with third through sixth grade students in the two neighborhood elementary schools explaining the purpose and details of the program, and describing Bryce and his special needs. The volunteer coordinator collected the response slips gathered by the volunteer representatives in each school and organized the master schedule. There was an overwhelming response from students interested in volunteering to read. Some children were very strong readers, while others were using this volunteer experience as an opportunity to work on improving their oral reading skills. No matter their reading level, they were all committed to doing their very best job when reading to Bryce.

Step Four: Discuss the Role of the Family and Professional (Educator/Administrator)

It is important that the professionals working with the family understand both the benefits of children developing friendships in their home and the challenges that parents face in facilitating such peer relationships (Geisthardt et al., 2002). Every family situation is unique. Depending on their individual interests and strengths, parents may assume some roles in facilitating their child's play opportunities and need support and assistance with others. For example, the family may need help in accessing and organizing peer volunteers as well as assistance in promoting the program on a regular basis in the schools. Effective home-based peer programs require the commitment of parents and professional educators, as well as other community members who may be key players in facilitating peer programs (Turnbull et al., 1999). Frank discussions regarding realistic levels of parental and professional involvement are critical to insuring the success of a home-based reading volunteer program.

Early on our family made a commitment to develop and implement this program because we felt it would be beneficial to Bryce's developmental progress. We saw this responsibility as no different than planning play dates for our other children. However, when the volunteer coordinator offered to provide administrative support, we were happy to accept. Bryce had only been home from the hospital for a few months and we were often overwhelmed by his medical care.

The success of this volunteer program is directly related to the support and encouragement of the administrators and educators in our local school system. In our case a comprehensive volunteer program with a funded coordinator existed because administrators, faculty, staff, and parents in our community are committed to volunteerism. From the beginning, the volunteer coordinator handled the paperwork, including disseminating the letter requesting volunteers, collecting the responses, and organizing the master schedule. The principals and teachers in our two neighborhood elementary schools encourage students to volunteer and formally recognize the students who participate. The support and guidance of professionals was key to the success of our program.

Step Five: Develop an Initial Orientation to Provide Information About the Child

A characteristic of successful social interaction programs is peer volunteer training that in part focuses on providing information about the child with severe disabilities, including communicative behavior and adaptive equipment (Hunt, Alwel, Farron-Davis, & Goetz, 1996; Staub & Hunt, 1993). An initial orientation for peers in a reading volunteer program may be conducted in a group or can occur one-on-one when peers arrive for their first visit. The training should focus on sharing information about the child's strengths and interests, communicative behavior, medical equipment, and adaptive devices. Strategies for reading to the child can be modeled during the orientation. Additionally, peers should be encouraged to ask questions or express concerns. The parents in the home supply supervision and additional information on a regular basis to facilitate positive social interactions.

We conduct an orientation for the children when they arrive for the first time in our home. Some children ask if their parents can stay, and we assure them that parents are always welcome. We introduce Bryce and his environment. Bryce's room is located in what had originally been the living and dining rooms of our home. The rooms are cheery and full of toys; however, there is no hiding the medical equipment. Bryce uses a tracheostomy tube for breathing and is seated in his wheelchair wearing a body brace. We talk to the children about why Bryce needs a special opening for breathing and how the thermovent filter "nose" fits over his tracheostomy tube. The "nose" works just like their nose, filtering and moisturizing the room air. If the "nose" falls off, we just put a new one back on. We briefly identify some of the more obvious medical equipment in the room, and take our cues from the children as to how much information to provide. Some children ask several questions, but most are initially more reticent. We encourage them to ask a question anytime, and assure them that every question is important. We underscore that an adult will always be in the home.

The next few minutes are spent discussing strategies to use when reading to Bryce. Bryce does not always use his eyes effectively, so we model how to hold a book in front of him to position the picture in his line of vision. We explain that Bryce uses his hearing to understand his world, and then we demonstrate using books with sounds that engage Bryce in the story. If the book has a page that is texturally interesting, we suggest the reader place Bryce's hand on the surface and explain what he is touching. We share how Bryce communicates what he likes by smiling and moving his arms. If more than one child volunteers to read in the same time slot, we explain that Bryce becomes confused by too much noise and suggest that they take turns reading and listening. The children start reading when they are ready, and we step back and allow the natural process of getting to know each other to begin.

Step Six: Supervise and Facilitate the Social Interaction Between Child and Peer

Successful social interactions between students with and without disabilities in inclusive classrooms are best supported by the direct intervention of the teacher (Hollingsworth, 2005; Odom & Brown, 1993). In the home, the parents must assume this role by actively facilitating the interaction process between their child and peers, which includes modeling strategies and providing feedback (Rosenberg & Boulware, 2005). Strategies for providing directed support and supervision during the social interaction include: (1) presenting the child and his/her environment in a strengths-based manner, (2) highlighting the child's interests and preferred sensory modality, (3) interpreting the child's communicative intent, (4) supporting peer-child interactions, and (5) providing peer feedback.

When the child with multiple disabilities is presented in a strengths-based manner by the family, peers will learn that the disability is an attribute that describes but does not define the child (Snow, 2003). For example, the parent may emphasize the child's skills and interests by saying; *"Bryce is very good at listening and he often smiles when he hears books with sound."* Peers will have questions about the child's special needs. These should be answered simply and honestly. For example, *"This is Bryce's thermovent filter 'nose' that fits over his tracheostomy tube. It works just like your nose; filtering and moisturizing the air he breathes."* Highlighting likenesses between the child and peers will be helpful as well (e.g., *"You brought your favorite book and that is one of Bryce's favorites too"*). Care should be taken that the child is dressed in clothing similar to peers, and that the physical environment where the interaction takes place is cheery with kid-friendly décor. Simple considerations such as having popular books to read and an assortment of adaptive toys available impart a warm, inviting atmosphere.

Highlighting the child's interests and preferred sensory modalities (Korsten, Dunn, Foss, & Francke, 1993) enables the reading experience to be more relevant to the peer and meaningful for the child. Parents can help peers select books that are the child's favorite types. For example, some children prefer books with sounds or repetitive phrases, while others respond best to books with bright pictures, flashing lights, or accompanying props. Peers can be shown how to place the hand of the child who prefers tactile sensations directly on texturally interesting pages or to use scratch and sniff books with the child who enjoys olfactory experiences. The area of the home selected for the reading interaction should be free of competitive environmental stimuli. Reducing extraneous conversation, turning the television off, and avoiding high traffic areas are especially important for the child prone to sensory over-stimulation.

Interpreting the child's communicative intent increases the likelihood of successful interactions between the child who is nonverbal and peers (Downing, 2002). This process begins when the adult provides the child a consistent cue to signal the peer-reading activity. The child's preferred sensory modality (auditory, visual, tactile) should guide the selection of the cue. For example, an auditory cue might use a simple phrase delivered with exaggerated intonation that begins by saying the child's name, while a visual cue could use a gesture or key word sign for book (Klein, Chen, & Haney, 2000). In addition to cuing the child, it is important to interpret the experience for the peer as well. Explain to the peer how the child without speech uses physical behaviors to communicate, such as a change in affect, motor movement, or eye gaze (Korsten et al., 1993). For example, *"Bryce, you are smiling so big, Charis and I can tell that you like this story."*

The adult best supports peer-child interactions by directing the focus toward the peer and child rather than the peer and adult. It is very easy when a child is nonverbal for meaningful communication and interaction to only occur between the peer and the adult. Redirect by interjecting the child into every conversation and activity, as well as teaching interaction skills to peers (Downing, 1999). For example, you can teach a method for offering a choice between two books selected by the peer: (1) hold each book separately in front of the child; (2) say the title; (3) pause and count slowly and silently to ten; (4) observe the child's physical response behaviors, such as change in affect or arm movement; and (5) respect communicative intent by reading the book that the child responds to in a positive manner. Always reinforce the peer for noticing the child's responses and attempts to communicate. Assistive technology can support the child to have a more active role in the reading activity (Downing, 2002). Prerecord texts of selected books into a voice output communication device with levels that can be activated by the child with a switch. In this way, the child and peer can take turns reading books together. Similarly, record a simple voice output communication device with a request that a book is read. The child can activate the device to ask the peer to read a book. Peers can be taught to inquire if the child wants a page of the book read, pause, and wait for the child to touch the device. The voice recorded into devices should be the same gender and age as the child.

The final strategy the adult can use to support social interactions is to provide peer feedback (Mastropieri & Scruggs, 2007). Point out when the child responds in a unique way and ask the peer if they noticed the response. Encourage the peer to share what they are learning from interactions with the child. Positive affirmations can reassure the peer that they are doing a great job. Feedback is most helpful if the adult is specific about the situation in which they observe the peer and child interacting in a particularly effective way. Likewise, if an incident occurs that is confusing to the peer, explain it in as simple and honest terms as possible.

During the first year of the program, Bryce was unresponsive. So we discussed with the children that we believed Bryce could hear our voices and would like some of his favorite picture books read. During the second year of the program, Bryce began to smile and cry in ways that were not always purposeful. We explained that sometimes Bryce cried for reasons that we did not understand and it had nothing to do with their reading. Once reassured, the children would continue reading the story while an adult stroked Bryce's face. Many times, we would notice the children reach over and compassionately pat Bryce's hand. Gradually, we noticed subtle improvements in Bryce. He became more responsive and started to smile and cry at appropriate times. As we learned to interpret his cues and signals, we explained to the peers how Bryce communicated by changing his facial affect and increasing his arm movements. During one boy's first visit with Bryce, we explained how to allow Bryce to choose a book. This young boy was very sincere in his attempt to offer Bryce a choice. As we moved out of sight, we listened but did not hear the boy begin reading. After a few minutes of silence, we walked over to them and saw a puzzled expression on the boy's face. He looked up and said very earnestly, "I am waiting, but his arms and face aren't telling me." We explained that this sometimes happens and what we do is tell Bryce that we especially like this book and then we make the choice ourselves. It has been a learning experience for everyone.

Step Seven: Implement a Communication Plan with Peers and Their Families

Implementing a communication plan insures that the volunteer program is efficient, manageable, and sensitive to the needs of the child and peers' families. A master schedule is crucial and everyone should have a copy. Include contact information for the child and peers with the schedule as well as the cancellation policy in the event of illness or schedule conflicts. Provide a sign-in form to document volunteer hours.

In our home we keep a sign-in sheet that has become a journal that the peers use to communicate with each other. Sometimes their comments are related to the books they are reading, while other times it is social conversation. The sign-in sheet became so cluttered with messages that we started providing 4x6 cards attached with a D-ring for the peers to write down messages. As they giggle and read the notes, Bryce follows their model and laughs too.

Step Eight: Promote, Advertise, and Nurture the Peer-Reading Program

Volunteer efforts flourish when they are promoted, advertised, and nurtured. This is best done by attending to the little details that affirm individual and organizational contributions. For example, (1) giving seasonal/holiday token gifts to peer readers, (2) donating a book to the venue providing volunteers, and (3) recognizing the children at local schools/community ceremonies let volunteers know that they are appreciated. Contact local media to encourage coverage of the reading volunteer program. Publicity rewards current participants and interests new ones in becoming involved.

We believe our volunteer program grows and flourishes each year because we nurture it and the participants. On a regular basis, we present small gifts (e.g., boxes of candy, gift certificates for an ice cream cone) as tokens of our appreciation of the children's commitment. We have made photo magnets from a picture taken of the volunteer reader with Bryce, so they can be displayed on peers' lockers or refrigerators. Yearly, we donate a book to the elementary school libraries in recognition of the students who read to Bryce. We also send a memo to the administrators of the two participating elementary schools that lists the student volunteers and highlights the special achievements of the program. Over the years, the volunteer reading program has been featured by local newspapers and filmed by two public broadcasting stations that aired on ZOOM, a nationally syndicated children's show. Publicity aside, we are certain that children choose to read to Bryce for reasons unrelated to rewards and recognition. As we remind them, Bryce's smile alone is a testament to how much he enjoys the books that are read to him and treasures the friendships he establishes with the children who read.

Step Nine: Evaluate the Success of the Program

Several methods can be used to evaluate the success of the program. Consider the benefits to the child, family, and peers. Since the focus of the program is the child, the evaluation system should document the child's response to social opportunities. Thoughtful reflection by the family through journaling or conversing with educators/administrators can note subtle changes that are observed in the child as a result of peer interactions and forge linkages between goals in the child's education program and outcomes of social opportunities in the home-based reading program. To document the effects on the family, regularly reflect on the benefits and challenges of the program. Educators and administrators can have a role in supporting the family in this effort, as well as brainstorming solutions to concerns. Finally, tracking the number and frequency of annual volunteer hours can substantiate a successful program or alert a pos-

Thoughtful reflection by the family through journaling or conversing with educators/administrators can note subtle changes that are observed in the child as a result of peer interactions and forge linkages between goals in the child's education program and outcomes of social opportunities in the home-based reading program.

sible concern. Check for peer satisfaction through informal conversations or more formal methods such as surveys.

In addition to providing multiple opportunities for auditory and visual stimulation, this program encourages Bryce to use communication skills. For example, Bryce uses his arms to indicate "more" of a preferred activity. Bryce generalizes this skill during social activity with friends in his home. Most importantly, the reading volunteer program provides Bryce increased opportunities to interact with peers, and the readers are like having a playmate come over to his house. Since each of the boys and girls who read has a distinct personality, Bryce learns to respond to different types of interaction styles with peers.

Conclusion

No program, regardless of its benefits, is without challenges. Our program involves children coming into our home, twice a day, six days a week. The frequency and quality of the social interactions between Bryce and his peers are integral to its success. However, the very features that characterize the program's value require commitment from the family. There have been times when we have had a long day and sigh as we think about a visit from a reader. Then we remember that we often have similar feelings when our other children entertain friends. The message is the same. Children with and without disabilities need friends. As parents, we accept this as part of our child-rearing responsibility.

The reading volunteer program has existed for 10 years. As might be expected, not every child who initially volunteers stays actively involved. Conflicting activities and lack of interest contribute to withdrawal from the program. To date, over 150 children have been invited into our home. They all enter as volunteer readers and many leave as friends. Program success is also measured through the words of those who participate. While the

children have noticed how Bryce is different from them, they often comment on the similarities, as one boy exclaimed, "Bryce, I have that same football shirt." Justin, who volunteers, asked to use Bryce as the focus of a research project he did this year in a program for children who are gifted and talented. The following are his words:

Many children initially read to Bryce because they think, "Poor kid, I should help him!" Sometimes it even takes a while to see past Bryce's disabilities and just see Bryce. But over time, the kids that read to Bryce start to see that people with disabilities are more like them than different. And many of the volunteers begin to look forward to not only reading to Bryce, but also simply getting to spend time with him. I have been reading to Bryce for over a year now, and I love it! Every time I go and see him, I enjoy watching him laugh when I sing to him, or after he knocks off his glasses purposefully. Bryce has a great personality and I love being able to spend time with him. It has been a life-changing experience for me!

The "specialness" of a program such as ours is that children discover they are more alike than different from each other, and learn to appreciate the uniqueness of every human being. Perhaps summing this program up best is Adam, who when asked why he reads to Bryce said, "I read to Bryce so that when he grows up he will read to his kids." Adam looks past Bryce's disabilities to see the child within. He calls him friend.

Notes
You can reach Kimberly A. Christensen by e-mail at kchris@bgsu.edu

References

Bishop, K. & Jubala, K. (1994). By June, given shared experiences, integrated classes, and equal opportunities, Jaime will have a friend. *Teaching Exceptional Children, 27*(1), 36-40.

Cole, D. A., Vandercook, T., & Rynders, J. (1988). Comparison of two peer interaction programs: Children with and without severe disabilities. *American Educational Research Journal, 25*(3), 415-439.

Downing, J. E. (1999). *Teaching communication skills to students with severe disabilities.* Baltimore: Paul H. Brookes.

Downing, J. E. (2002). *Including students with severe and multiple disabilities in typical classrooms: Practical strategies for teachers* (2nd ed.). Baltimore: Paul H. Brookes.

Evans, I. M., Salisbury, C. L., Palombaro, M. M., Berryman, J., & Hollowood, T. M. (1992). Peer interactions and social acceptance of elementary-age children with severe disabilities in an inclusive school. *Journal of the Association for Persons with Severe Handicaps, 17*, 205-212.

Forest, M. & Lusthaus, E. (1989). Promoting educational equality for all students: Circles and maps. In S. Stainback, W. Stainback, & M. Forest (Eds.), *Educating all students in the mainstream of regular education* (pp. 43-57). Baltimore: Paul H. Brookes.

Geisthardt, C. L., Brotherson, M. J., & Cook, C. C. (2002). Friendships of children with disabilities in the home environment. *Education and Training in Mental Retardation and Developmental Disabilities, 37*(3), 235-252.

Giangreco, M. F., Cloninger, C. J., Dennis, R. E., & Edelman, S. W. (2000). Problem-solving methods to facilitate inclusive education. In R. A. Villa & J. S. Thousand (Eds.), *Restructuring for caring and effective education: Piecing the puzzle together* (2nd ed., pp. 293-327). Baltimore: Paul H. Brookes.

Guralnick, M. J. (1999). The nature and meaning of social integration for young children with mild developmental delays in inclusive settings. *Journal of Early Intervention, 22*, 70-86.

Hendrickson, J. M., Shokoohi-Yekta, M., Hamre-Nietupski, S., & Gable, R. (1996). Middle and high school students' perceptions on being friends with peers with severe disabilities. *Exceptional Children, 63*, 19-28.

Hollingsworth, H. L. (2005). Interventions to promote peer social interactions in preschool settings. *Young Exceptional Children, 9*(1), 2-11.

Hughes, C., Guth, C., Hall, S., Presley, J., Dye, M., & Byers, C. (1999). They are my best friends: Peer buddies promote inclusion in high school. *Teaching Exceptional Children, 31*(5), 32-37.

Hunt, P., Alwell, M., Farron-Davis, F., & Goetz, L. (1996). Creating socially supportive environments for fully included students who experience multiple disabilities. *Journal of the Association for Persons with Severe Handicaps, 21*, 53-71.

Klein, M.D., Chen, D., & Haney, M. (2000). *Promoting learning through active interaction: A guide to early communication with young children who have multiple disabilities.* Baltimore: Paul H. Brookes.

Korsten, J.E., Dunn, D.K., Foss, T.V., & Francke, M.K. (1993). Every move counts: *Sensory-based communication techniques.* San Antonio, TX: Therapy Skill Builders.

Mastropieri, M. A. & Scruggs, T. E. (2007). *The inclusive classroom: Strategies for effective instruction* (3rd ed.). Upper Saddle River, NJ: Pearson Education.

National Scientific Council on the Developing Child: Working Paper No. 2. (2004). *Children's emotional development is built into the architecture of their brain.* Retrieved February 25, 2006 from http://www.developingchild.net/reports.shtml

Odom, S. J. & Brown, W. H. (1993). Social interaction skills interventions for young children with disabilities in integrated settings. In C. A. Peck, S. L. Odom, & D. D. Bricker (Eds.). *Integrating young children with disabilities into community programs: Ecological perspectives on research and implementations* (pp. 39-64). Baltimore: Paul H. Brooks.

Rosenberg, N. & Boulware, G. L. (2005). Playdates for young children with autism and other disabilities. *Young Exceptional Children, 8*(2), 11-20.

Salisbury, C., Gallucci, C., Palombaro, M. M., & Peck, C. A. (1995). Strategies that promote social relations among elementary students with and without severe disabilities in inclusive schools. *Exceptional Children, 62*, 125-137.

Sandall, S., Hemmeter, M. L., Smith, B. J., & McLean, M. E. (2005). *DEC recommended* practices: A comprehensive guide for practical application in early intervention/early childhood special education. Longmont, CO: Sopris West.

Snow, K. (2003). *People first language.* Retrieved February 25, 2006 from http://www.disabilityisnatural.com

Staub, D. & Hunt, P. (1993). The effects of social interaction training on high school peer tutors of schoolmates with severe disabilities. *Exceptional Children, 60*, 41-57.

Strully, J. & Strully, C. (1985). Friendships and our children. *Journal of the Association for Persons with Severe Handicaps, 10*, 224-227.

Turnbull, A. P., Pereira, L., & Blue-Banning, M. J. (1999). Parents' facilitation of friendships between their children with a disability and friends without a disability. *Journal of the Association for Persons with Severe Handicaps, 24*, 85-99.

Vandercook, T., York, J., & Forest, M. (1989). The McGill Action Planning System (MAPS): A strategy for building the vision. *Journal of the Association for Persons with Severe Handicaps, 14,* 205-215.

Family Perceptions of Challenging Behavior

Strategies for Providing Effective Supports

Amanda L. Tyrrell, M.Ed.,
University of Kansas

Rachel Freeman, Ph.D.,
University of Kansas

Cynthia R. Chambers, M.Ed.,
University of Kansas

Children with disabilities can add a challenging, yet rewarding dynamic to the family system. When these children exhibit challenging behavior, families may be faced with a whole new set of stressors. Though challenging behavior, sometimes referred to as problem behavior, varies from child to child, it can affect parents, siblings, and the functioning of the entire family (Fox, Vaughn, Wyatte, & Dunlap, 2002). Children engage in challenging behavior in a variety of ways and the intensity of these behaviors varies significantly. Challenging behavior can take many forms, from disruptive behavior such as tantrums, aggression to others, and property destruction to more isolated behaviors such as social withdrawal or self-stimulatory behaviors (Bambara, 2005). Challenging behavior, no matter the intensity, can be very problematic for families.

Bambara (2005) affirms that challenging behavior is defined by its effect on the child and the systems around the child. The child and his or her family and the preschool program, school, or community contexts where the child participates, in part determine what constitutes challenging behavior. In other words, challenging behavior is defined by the culture in which it occurs and becomes a challenging behavior when it is perceived by the culture as impeding social and emotional development. Though some challenging behavior is exhibited by typically developing children, especially young children, the effect of these behaviors on the child's life is the important aspect (Lucyshyn, Horner, Dunlap, Albin, & Ben, 2002).

Given that challenging behavior has an impact on children as well as families, understanding challenging behavior in the context of families is critical. Taking a family-focused approach is essential for professionals who are trying to understand and address these behaviors (Lucyshyn et al., 2002). Sensitivity to cultural perspectives becomes an essential part of the assessment process for understanding why a child is engaging in certain behaviors (Chen, Downing, & Peckham-Hardin, 2002; Salend & Taylor, 2002). The effectiveness of assessment and intervention planning is therefore strongly influenced by the team of family, professional, and community members who are working together to develop strategies that will prevent and address the function of a child's challenging behavior.

Professionals who are effective at facilitating these multidisciplinary teams pay attention to the perceptions, emotional well-being, and cultural background of the children, their families, and other individuals providing support (Lucyshyn et al., 2002). In fact, facilitators who are sensitive to a family's social and emotional needs may be more successful in providing the supports needed to improve the quality of life for an entire family (Blue-Banning, Summers, Frankland, Nelson, & Beegle, 2004). This article will highlight team-based strategies and characteristics that can help teams become more sensitive to the social and emotional issues both children and families experience. The purpose of this paper is to (1) describe the impact of children's challenging behavior on families, (2) discuss supports that have been found to be beneficial for families, and (3) determine effective strategies for facilitators working with families of children with challenging behavior. By effectively identifying supports for children with challenging behavior, we can improve the overall quality of life for the entire family.

Impact of Challenging Behavior

As professionals develop partnerships with families to address challenging behavior, they need a firm understanding of how the challenging behaviors impact the child's family system as well as the greater community in which the child and his or her family participate. Being sensitive to family members' perspectives and having knowledge about how the family experiences challenging behavior helps to prepare professionals to partner with families. This section will highlight parental perspectives of challenging behavior as they relate to the entire family (e.g., parents, siblings, grandparents) and the communities (e.g., preschool, childcare, school, grocery store, community recreational options, religious organizations) in which the child and family participate.

Impact on Family Subsystems

Challenging behavior can have substantial and lasting effects on members of the family, including the child with a disability, the parents, siblings, and extended family (Fox, Vaughn, Dunlap, & Bucy, 1997). The lifestyle of families can be dramatically changed when children engage in these behaviors, since the difficulties that arise result in a "24-hour, 7-day involvement" (Fox et al., 2002, p. 443). Families report feeling that there are constant demands upon them to support and advocate for their children (Turnbull & Ruef, 1996). These challenges can alter activities in which the family participates and may result in social isolation for the family (Fox et al., 1997). Other mental health issues may compound problems that family members experience including depression, illness, or poverty, which influence the family dynamics and overall functioning (Markey, Markey, Quant, Santelli, & Turnbull, 2002; Singer, Goldberg-Hamblin, Peckham-Hardin, Barry, & Santarelli, 2002; Turnbull & Turnbull, 1999).

Families report feeling that there are constant demands upon them to support and advocate for their children (Turnbull & Ruef, 1996).

Challenging behavior can result in a number of social and emotional stressors for families. Qualitative studies that focus on parental perceptions of challenging behavior have identified a number of emotional experience stressors, including (1) feeling that professionals, extended family members, and individuals within the community are judging or blaming the parent for the child's behavior; (2) worrying that siblings are being negatively impacted by a brother or sister's challenging behaviors; and (3) experiencing the feeling that parents must act as advocates and service coordinators to ensure their children are included in everyday school and community settings (Blue-Banning et al., 2004; Dunlap, Robbins, & Darrow, 1994; Fox et al., 1997; Fox et al., 2002; Park & Turnbull, 2002; Ruef, Turnbull, Turnbull, & Poston, 1999; Turnbull & Ruef, 1996, 1997).

Parents. Parents are often the most affected by their children's challenging behavior, and these behaviors may serve as a stressor in their lives. Children's behavior may be difficult to handle or dangerous to themselves or others and as a result, parents may frequently worry about these challenging behaviors occurring (Turnbull & Ruef, 1996). In addition to these feelings, parents sometimes feel that professionals blame the child or the family members for the occurrences of challenging behaviors. Some parents perceive professionals as holding them responsible for their child's challenging behaviors. Parents may receive phone calls from a variety of

■■■■■■■■■■■■■■■■■■

Parents sometimes feel that pro-
fessionals blame the child or the
family members for the occur-
rences of challenging behaviors.

service providers describing behavioral episodes, which may leave them feeling overwhelmed and powerless (Turnbull & Turnbull, 1999).

Within their extended families, parents may feel blamed by and isolated from their family members. Extended family members may not understand the child's disability and believe that the behaviors are related to ineffective parental discipline (Turnbull & Ruef, 1996, 1997). However, parents often meet a supportive professional or family member that they describe as special who puts them at ease.

Siblings. When a brother or sister engages in challenging behavior, parents report that siblings experience a number of emotions. Siblings may experience anger towards their brother or sister who exhibits challenging behavior (Fox et al., 1997), or be embarrassed or angry that the child with challenging behavior receives more attention than they do (Turnbull & Ruef, 1997). In addition, challenging behavior can be frightening for all family members, including siblings (Fox et al., 1997). Many children miss the opportunity to engage in activities with their brother or sister who engages in challenging behavior. Although challenging behavior can evoke negative feelings within siblings, many children may actually learn to be more patient and responsible when they have a family member with challenging behavior (Turnbull & Ruef, 1997).

Impact on Participation in the Community

Children with disabilities and, more specifically, those who engage in challenging behavior are often excluded from living as other children do, going to school, and participating in community activities. Therefore, opportunities for school and community inclusion may be limited. The following sections will examine the perspectives of parents with respect to school and community inclusion.

Preschool/School Inclusion. When children exhibit challenging behavior, parents may find themselves assuming roles outside of basic parenting, such as an advocate and intervener (Turnbull & Ruef, 1997). In fact, family members are often the main advocate and service coordinator for the child (Turnbull & Turnbull, 1999). Parents of children who engage in challenging behavior sometimes perceive that the program their child attends is not in compliance with the Individuals with Disabilities Education Act (IDEA) (Turnbull & Ruef, 1997). In some cases, the child may be placed in a more restrictive setting than the parent believes is necessary. If the program is out of compliance with these legal

Table 1
Resources for PCP

Learn More about Person-Centered Planning
PACER Center—Parent Advocacy Coalition for Educational Rights (http://www.pacer.org)
The PACER Center provides information from families to other families of children with disabilities to improve their quality of life. The website contains articles on such topics as person-centered planning, transition, early childhood, and emotional/behavioral disorders and provides translated materials. Links to additional online resources are also provided.
Institute for Community Inclusion (http://www.communityinclusion.org)
The Institute for Community Inclusion is an organization that supports individuals with disabilities in the community. Their website includes articles about person-centered planning and involving individuals with disabilities in the PCP process and work placements.
MPACT—Parent Training and Information (http://www.ptimpact.com)
This website provides training modules on five areas of transition planning including person-centered planning. They provide information to families of children with disabilities, organizations, and advocacy groups both online and through training sessions throughout the state of Missouri.
Kansas Institute for Positive Behavior Support Online Library (http://www.kipbs.org/Library/default.aspx)
This program received Medicaid funds to provide training to professionals on implementing person-centered planning with individuals they serve. The training materials available on this website are intended to support families and professionals working with children and adults who engage in challenging behavior to improve their overall quality of life.
Beach Center on Disability (http://www.beachcenter.org/)
The Beach Center website provides a number of resources including research articles, newsletters, anecdotal stories, and presentations on topics such as person-centered planning. Additional information on Group Action Planning, a person-centered planning process, can be found on this website.

requirements, parents are placed in a position of advocating for their child's rights (Turnbull & Ruef, 1996, 1997).

As part of their advocacy role, parents may participate in activities for improving their child's success in inclusive settings at school. For instance, they may be invited by the program staff to talk to typically developing peers about their child in order to facilitate peers' understanding of the child and his or her behaviors (Turnbull & Ruef, 1997). Many families believe that including their children in neighborhood school and com-

Table 2
Online Resources for PBS

Learn More about Positive Behavior Support
Center on the Social and Emotional Foundation for Early Learning (http://csefel.uiuc.edu/)
This is a national center focused on strengthening the capacity of child care and Head Start programs to improve the social and emotional outcomes of young children. Go to the menu at the top of the page and find the link labeled "Resources".
Center for Evidence-based Practice (http://challengingbehavior.fmhi. usf.edu/index.html)
The Center for Evidence-Based Practice: Young Children with Challenging Behavior is funded by the Office of Special Education Programs and is intended to raise awareness and implementation of positive, evidence-based practices.
Kansas Institute for Positive Behavior Support Online Library (http://www.kipbs.org/Library/default.aspx)
This program received Medicaid funds to provide training on positive behavior support. The training materials available on this website are intended to support families and professionals working with children and adults who engage in challenging behavior.
Online Academy Positive Behavior Support Modules (http://uappbs. apbs.org/)
This website contains a set of modules that describe how to create an individual positive behavior support plan in school settings.
Association for Positive Behavior Support (http://www.apbs.org/main.htm)
This is the website for the International Association for Positive Behavior Support (APBS). APBS is dedicated to the advancement of positive behavior support and is made up of professionals, family members, trainers, consumers, researchers, and administrators who come together annually to share information and learn more about positive behavior support.
OSEP National Technical Assistance Center on Positive Behavioral Interventions and Supports (PBIS) (www.pbis.org)
This center is funded by the Office of Special Education Programs (OSEP) to give schools capacity-building information and technical assistance for identifying, adapting, and sustaining effective school-wide disciplinary practices.

munity settings can provide important opportunities for their children to learn appropriate behavior from their peers and help develop social-emotional competence. When children with disabilities are included with peers, friendships can develop that may otherwise be difficult to foster (Turnbull & Turnbull, 1999).

Challenging behavior can become a barrier between children and their peers, which may lead to damage of new or established friendships (Turnbull & Turnbull, 1999). Parents fear their children will exhibit challenging behavior, such as aggression towards peers at school (Turnbull & Ruef, 1996, 1997). As a result of challenging behavior and a lack of appropriate social-emotional skills, many children do not have friendships, which affect both the child and the parents. In addition, a lack of friendships can impact a child and family's sense of belonging in school settings. Many parents see building positive friendships as a necessity (Turnbull & Turnbull, 1999); however, they may not feel comfortable facilitating and fostering these relationships (Turnbull & Ruef, 1997). Parents desire a means to address their concerns for their child's social development without feeling as though the promotion of friendships rests solely on their shoulders.

Community Inclusion. The number of outings in the community with the child may be limited due to challenging behavior or families may opt not to venture into the community at all (Fox et al., 1997). To avoid the occurrence of challenging behavior, parents may run errands or participate in the community without the child or when he or she is in school. When challenging behavior occurs, parents may avoid going out in the community, which results in the family remaining in their own home a great deal of the time. Vacations can be difficult for families due to the change in routine and dissimilarity of the vacation spot with home; therefore, they may also be avoided (Turnbull & Ruef, 1997).

Parents are often anxious about challenging behavior occurring in a public setting. For example, a family reported by Fox and colleagues (1997) only goes into the community when it is not crowded and sings to the child with challenging behavior to keep him busy. They worry about how the challenging behavior will affect the child and each member of the family in the community setting (Turnbull & Ruef, 1996). Additionally, they do not want other people in the community to be disrupted (Turnbull & Ruef, 1997). Sometimes parents fear behaviors that have never happened before because they are so worried of what could happen. Helping parents and family members cope with this type of anxiety is important and will create a context for change.

Team-Based Strategies and Supports for Families

The social and emotional context of a family's response to challenging behavior must be considered before a team can move to assessment and problem-solving activities. The next section of this paper will describe two team-based strategies that can be used to support children who engage in challenging behavior and their families (i.e., person-centered planning and positive behavior support).

Person-Centered Planning

Person-centered planning (PCP) is a team-based process that allows the team, including the focus individual as appropriate, to build on an individual's strengths and preferences and to create goals and visions for the future (Kincaid, 1996). These goals are created to help children and families improve their quality of life and build on a child's social and emotional strengths within a collaborative team context (Albin, Lucyshyn, Horner, & Flannery, 1996). Most PCP plans include the development of a circle or network of support around a child who meet regularly and use natural or community supports to achieve the preferred lifestyle (Turnbull et al., 1996).

PCP begins by discussing the individual's history, strengths, and accomplishments over time and focuses on the preferences and dreams of the individual (Butterworth, Steere, & Whitney-Thomas, 1997). A facilitator assists the individual, his or her family members, and other team members in the planning process and in focusing on the individual through creative problem solving (Turnbull et al., 1996). Next, the individual's lifestyle preferences and vision for the future are determined with as much input from the individual as possible. As goals are created to reach the preferred lifestyle, team members are enrolled to begin implementing first steps towards reaching that goal. Additional team meeting times are set to ensure that the process continues and does not end after the initial meeting. For more information on PCP, see Table 1 for online resources.

Positive Behavior Support

Positive behavior support (PBS) refers to a number of research-based strategies that are assessment-based and that combine the science of behavior and information about physical and mental health with person-centered values in order to increase quality of life and decrease challenging behaviors (Horner, 2000; Horner, Sugai, Todd, & Lewis-Palmer, 2005). PBS is focused on providing lasting and sustainable outcomes for individuals with challenging behavior and their families (Horner, Albin, Sprague, & Todd, 2000) and is based on the components of applied behavior analysis (Baer, Wolf, & Risley, 1968). An essential part of the PBS process is to create active family member and team involvement in the assessment of challenging behavior and the implementation of strategies for teaching social and emotional development skills and changing problematic routines and settings to limit the challenging behaviors (Lucyshyn et al., 2002). A PBS plan must be a good fit for the family and other team members who will be implementing the PBS plan (Albin et al., 1996). This means that the family and team members believe that the plan reflects the values of the team and is easy and efficient to carry out given the skills and resources of those using the PBS plan.

An essential part of the PBS process is to create active family member and team involvement in the assessment of challenging behavior and the implementation of strategies for teaching social and emotional development skills and changing problematic routines and settings to limit the challenging behaviors (Lucyshyn et al., 2002).

A functional behavior assessment, including both direct and indirect measures, is conducted to determine the possible functions of the problem behavior (O'Neill et al., 1997). Once a hypothesized function or functions are determined, the positive behavior support plan can be developed with input from the entire team. Ongoing monitoring of the plan and implementing revisions as needed are vital for its success. For online resources leading to further information on PBS, see Table 2.

Summary of PCP and PBS

The purpose of both PCP and PBS is to increase the quality of life of both the child and the family (Kincaid, 1996; Horner, 2000). Both children with and without disabilities can benefit from the PCP and PBS process. Teams develop goals/outcomes through the person-centered planning process that can be reached through PBS. For example, increasing the child's participation in certain community activities and decreasing challenging behavior may be targeted goals. Person-centered planning provides critical information that can be used during the functional behavior assessment and provides a vision for the team throughout the PBS process (Kincaid, 1996). For that reason, PCP should be conducted before or concurrently with the PBS process. Each process improves the effectiveness of the other (Kincaid & Fox, 2002). Though these approaches demand considerable time and emotional and physical energy from families, the impact it has on families can be life altering.

Table 3
Strategies to Support Families of Children With Challenging Behavior

Parents say that professionals should:
• Develop their knowledge and understanding of the feelings and judgement or blame that families experience when a child engages in challenging behavior and thus be more sensitive to family members during meetings
• Acknowledge the family's feelings of needing to serve as advocate and service coordinator for their child and use the team process to share some of those responsibilities
• Actively connect families to family support groups and advocacy organizations as a part of the PBS process to decrease feelings of isolation
• Spend time learning about a family's culture and learn how those beliefs have the potential to influence decisions made by both the family and other members of the team during problem solving sessions
• Include strategies for supporting siblings within the PBS plan so that they receive time and attention as well from the family
• Work as a team in partnership with families to support children with disabilities in developing friendships by creating opportunities for peer contact, teaching social skills, and setting the stage for positive interactions with other children
• Focus on child strengths and build on existing skills

Incorporating Family Perceptions in Team-Based Strategies

Person-centered planning and positive behavior support strategies will be more effective if professionals are sensitive to the family perceptions of challenging behavior discussed in this article. See Table 3 for strategies to support families of children with challenging behavior. Understanding family perceptions can create a positive atmosphere for social and emotional growth during both person-centered and positive behavior support planning, not only for the child but the child's team as well.

Professionals and community members who are aware of the feelings of judgment or blame that families experience when a child engages in challenging behavior may be more sensitive to family members during meetings. Actively helping parents connect to family support groups and family advocacy organizations as a part of the PBS process may decrease feelings of isolation (Turnbull & Turnbull, 2001). By empowering families to advocate for their children, professionals build trusting relationships with families in a supportive team context (Blue-Banning et al., 2004).

To work effectively with others in a culturally sensitive manner involves first knowing yourself, your beliefs, and your values (Turnbull & Turnbull, 2001). It is important to understand that the values held by families may vary greatly from culture to culture, and more specifically family to family. Families may also differ on their level of acceptance of the disability (Chen et al., 2002). By gathering information about the family system and the culture of the family, professionals can learn more about the practices and beliefs of each family and may conduct their practices with families in a more respectful manner (Blue-Banning et al., 2004). Since the majority of professionals are of the mainstream culture and view challenging behavior in that context, they should strive to resolve differences that may exist between their ideas and the ideas of families (Chen et al., 2002). By being culturally sensitive when providing PBS, the process will "fit" better with the family's values and expectations.

A team may include goals/outcomes and activities within a PBS plan to support the brother or sister of a child who engages in challenging behavior. Creating plans to teach siblings ways to cope with fear or anxiety, as well as prevent and respond to challenging behavior could be included as part of the PBS plan. In other cases, the team may brainstorm ways to make sure that siblings obtain positive attention for appropriate behavior and special opportunities to balance the attention being received as part of a brother or sister's PBS plan. Professionals should model positive approaches with children rather than focusing on a child's deficits (Fox et al., 2002). Overall, there are a number of qualities that promote a successful partnership between families and professionals in the field. By becoming more sensitive to the experiences of parents and families, we can better support the children we work with who engage in challenging behavior.

Part of effectively preventing a child's challenging behavior involves creating a collaborative partnership with families and becoming sensitive to their needs. These relationships take time and energy, though in comparison to other interventions, this process seems quite cost-beneficial (Blue-Banning et al., 2004). A successful partnership between families and professionals is necessary and should encompass certain professional qualities, including the willingness to encourage and support communication-effective strategies (Blue-Banning et al., 2004). Person-centered planning

By becoming more sensitive to the experiences of parents and families, we can better support the children we work with who engage in challenging behavior.

and positive behavior support are two examples of team-based processes that assist teams in focusing on a child's strengths and build social and emotional skills. Incorporating information from the literature about family perceptions of challenging behavior will set the stage for successful PCP and PBS plans.

Conclusion

When providing services it is important that professionals look at the child and the whole family system as interventions are developed and implemented through team-based strategies, such as person-centered planning and positive behavior support. It is important to realize that families are not simply dealing with challenging behavior on a regular basis. They are also learning to handle a variety of emotional fears and social criticisms. Though challenging behaviors may be problematic, two team-based strategies (i.e., person-centered planning and positive behavior support) were discussed that parents and research have determined to be effective. By looking into the qualitative literature on families' perceptions of challenging behavior, professionals can begin to understand the underlying issues and create supportive relationships. In creating these collaborative relationships with families and implementing best practice interventions, such as positive behavior support, we can better support families of children with challenging behavior.

Note
You can reach Amanda Tyrrell by email at alt@ku.edu

References
Albin, R. W., Lucyshyn, J. M., Horner, R. H., & Flannery, K. B. (1996). Contextual fit for behavioral support plans: A model for "goodness of fit." In L. K. Koegel, R. L. Koegel, & G. Dunlap (Eds.), *Positive behavioral support: Including people with difficult behavior in the community* (pp. 81-98). Baltimore: Paul H. Brookes.

Baer, D. M., Wolf, M. M., & Risley, T. R. (1968). Current dimensions of applied behavior analysis. *Journal of Applied Behavior Analysis, 1*, 91-97.

Bambara, L. M. (2005). Evolution of positive behavior support. In L. M. Bambara & L. Kern (Eds.), *Individualized supports for students with challenging behaviors: Designing positive behavior plans* (pp. 1-24). New York: Guilford Press.

Blue-Banning, M., Summers, J. A., Frankland, H. C., Nelson, L. L., & Beegle, G. (2004). Dimensions of family and professional partnerships: Constructive guidelines for collaboration. *Exceptional Children, 70*, 167-184.

Butterworth, J., Steere, D., & Whitney-Thomas, J. (1997). Using person-centered planning to address personal quality of life. In R. Schalock (Ed.), *Quality of life: Vol. II Application to persons with disabilities* (pp. 5-23). Washington, DC: American Association on Mental Retardation.

Chen, D., Downing, J. E., & Peckham-Hardin, K. D. (2002). Working with families of diverse cultural and linguistic backgrounds: Considerations for culturally responsive positive behavior supports. In J. M. Lucyshyn, G. Dunlap, and R. W. Albin (Eds.), *Families and positive behavior support: Addressing challenging behavior in family contexts* (pp. 133-151). Baltimore: Paul H. Brookes.

Dunlap, G., Robbins, F. R., & Darrow, M. A. (1994). Parents' reports of their children's challenging behaviors: Results of a statewide survey. *Mental Retardation, 32*, 206-212.

Fox, L., Vaughn, B. J., Dunlap, G., & Bucy, M. (1997). Parent-professional partnership in behavioral support: A qualitative analysis of one family's experience. *The Journal of the Association for Persons with Severe Handicaps, 22*, 198-207.

Fox, L., Vaughn, B. J., Wyatte, M. L., & Dunlap, G. (2002). "We can't expect other people to understand": Family perspectives on challenging behavior. *Exceptional Children, 68,* 437-450.

Horner, R. H. (2000). Positive behavior supports. *Focus on Autism and Other Developmental Disabilities, 15*(2), 97-105.

Horner, R. H., Albin, R. W., Sprague, J. R., & Todd, A. (2000). Positive behavior support. In M. E. Snell & F. Brown (Eds.), *Instruction of students with severe disabilities* (pp. 207-243). Upper Saddle River, NJ: Merrill.

Horner, R. H., Sugai, G., Todd, A. W., & Lewis-Palmer, T. (2005). Schoolwide positive behavior support. In L. M. Bambara & L. Kern, (Eds.) *Individualized supports for students with problem behaviors: Designing positive behavior plans.* (pp. 359-390). New York: Guilford Press.

Individuals with Disabilities Education Act (IDEA) Amendments of 1997, PL 105-17, 20 U.S.C. [section] 1400 et seq.

Kincaid, D. (1996). Person-centered planning. In L. K. Koegel, R. L. Koegel, & G. Dunlap (Eds.), *Positive behavioral support: Including people with difficult behavior in the community* (pp. 439-465). Baltimore: Paul H. Brookes.

Kincaid, D. & Fox, L. (2002). Person-centered planning and positive behavior support. In S. Holburn & P. Vietze (Eds.), *Person-centered planning: Research, practice, and future directions* (pp. 29-49). Baltimore: Paul H. Brookes.

Lucyshyn, J. M., Horner, R. H., Dunlap, G., Albin, R.W., & Ben, K. R. (2002). Positive behavior support with families. In J. M. Lucyshyn, G. Dunlap, & R. W. Albin (Eds.), *Families and Positive Behavior Support: Addressing challenging behavior in family contexts* (pp. 3-44). Baltimore: Paul H. Brookes.

Markey, U., Markey, D. J., Quant, B, Santelli, B., & Turnbull, A. P. (2002). Operation positive change: PBS in an urban context. *Journal of Positive Behavior Interventions, 4,* 218-230.

O'Neill, R. E., Horner, R. H., Albin, R. W., Sprague, J. R., Storey, K., & Newton, J. S. (1997). *Functional assessment and program development for problem behavior: A practical handbook* (2nd ed.). Pacific Grove, CA: Brookes/Cole.

Park, J. & Turnbull, A. P. (2002). Quality indicators of professionals who work with children with challenging behavior. *Journal of Positive Behavior Interventions, 4,* 118-122.

Ruef, M. B., Turnbull, A. P., Turnbull, H. R., & Poston, D. (1999). Perspectives of five stakeholder groups: Challenging behavior of individuals with mental retardation and/or autism. *Journal of Positive Behavior Interventions, 1,* 43-58.

Salend, S. J. & Taylor, L. S. (2002). Cultural perspectives: Missing pieces in the functional assessment process. *Intervention in School and Clinic, 38*(2), 104-112

Singer, G. H., Goldberg-Hamblin, S. E., Peckham-Hardin, K. D., Barry, L., & Santarelli, G. E. (2002). Toward a synthesis of family support practices and positive behavior support. In J. M. Lucyshyn, G. Dunlap, & R. W. Albin (Eds.), *Families and positive behavior support: Addressing challenging behavior in family contexts* (pp. 155-183). Baltimore: Paul H. Brookes.

Turnbull, A. P., Blue-Banning, M. J., Anderson, E. L., Turnbull, H. R., Seaton, K. A., & Dinas, P. A. (1996). Enhancing self-determination through group action planning: A holistic emphasis. In D. Sands & M. Wehmeyer (Eds.), *Self-determination across the lifespan: Independence and choice for people with disabilities* (pp.237-256). Baltimore: Paul H. Brookes.

Turnbull, A. P. & Ruef, M. B. (1996). Family perspectives on challenging behavior. *Mental Retardation, 34,* 280-293.

Turnbull, A. P. & Ruef, M. B. (1997). Family perspectives on inclusive lifestyle issues for people with challenging behavior. *Exceptional Children, 63,* 221-227.

Turnbull, A. P. & Turnbull, H. R. (1999). Comprehensive lifestyle support for adults with challenging behavior: From rhetoric to reality. *Education and Training in Mental Retardation and Developmental Disabilities, 34,* 373-394.

Turnbull, A. P. & Turnbull, H. R. (2001). *Families, professionals and exceptionality: Collaboration for empowerment* (4th ed.). Upper Saddle River, NJ: Prentice Hall.

Aggression? Using Positive Behavior Support to Address Challenging Behavior

Lise Fox, Ph.D.,
University of South Florida

Shelley Clarke, M.A.,
University of South Florida

Cooper is a bright-eyed 2½-year-old boy, who is curious and full of energy. He is receiving early intervention services (through Infant Toddler/Part C of IDEA) due to communication delays and behavioral concerns and attends a community preschool program for part of the day. His problem behaviors often begin in the morning during the play period that occurs as children are arriving. He wanders aimlessly in the classroom and then frequently initiates an aggressive interaction with a peer. The aggressive behavior is quite intense, taking the form of biting, hitting, tackling, pinching, and head-butting and continues until the teacher separates Cooper from the other child or the child runs away. On quite a few occasions, Cooper will chase the child and continue the aggression. Cooper's aggressive behavior threatens the safety of the other children, causes great concern among the parents of children who have been attacked by Cooper, and causes the staff of the program to question their ability to continue to enroll Cooper. The teachers have tried a number of strategies to reduce the aggressive behavior without much success. The preschool director shares, "He has stolen my heart, we all love him here." But she also acknowledges that the current method for addressing Cooper's aggressive behavior in the classroom is not working, and unless his aggressive behavior can be controlled, she will be forced to ask his parents to withdraw him from the preschool.

Recent national newspaper headlines have noted the distressing news that young children are being expelled from state-funded preschool programs at rates that exceed public schools that enroll children in grades kindergarten through 12 (e.g., *Washington Post* [Dobbs, 2005], *USA Today* [della Cava, 2005], *New York Times* [Lewin, 2005]). These data confirm what many early educators and program directors already know—many young children come to preschool with aggression that is non-responsive to traditional classroom guidance procedures and poses a safety risk to other children. The sad outcome for many children, their families, and programs is that children are asked to leave.

Preschool aggression is not a rare phenomenon. Many young children use aggression to communicate their needs and wants and may use hitting, biting, and throwing objects as a mechanism to gain or escape attention or an object/activity (Coie & Dodge, 1998). In most cases, early educators are able to guide the child to use more appropriate behavior and the incidents of aggression quickly diminish. However, some children display aggressive behaviors at levels—both in number and intensity—that are not responsive to commonly practiced child guidance procedures. Based on a review of prevalence studies, Campbell (1995) estimated that 10%–15% of young children have mild to moderate behavior problems.

Many young children come to preschool with aggression that is non-responsive to traditional classroom guidance procedures and poses a safety risk to other children.

Early-appearing aggressive behavior does and should cause early educators great concern. Research indicates that early-appearing aggressive behavior has a good likelihood of persisting during the school years and continuing into adolescence (Campbell, 1995; Egeland, Kalkoske, Gottesman, & Erickson, 1990; Pierce, Ewing, & Campbell, 1999). Problem behavior that occurs during preschool is the single best predictor of adolescent delinquency, gang membership, and incarceration (Dishion, French, & Patterson, 1995; Reid, 1993).

Positive Behavior Support (PBS) offers a promising intervention approach for addressing aggressive behavior (Fox, Dunlap, & Cushing, 2002; Fox, Dunlap, & Powell, 2002). PBS is based on the assumption that children engage in challenging behavior to gain or escape access to attention, objects, or activities (O'Neill et al., 1997). Thus, problem behavior has a function or purpose. The general intervention approach used in PBS is to identify the function of the behavior and then teach the child new skills to replace the problem behavior. The use of PBS is supported by a growing body of literature that provides evidence of the effectiveness of this approach with children and adults of all ages and varied disabilities or delays (Carr et al., 1999; Conroy, Dunlap, Clarke, & Alter, 2005).

This article describes the use of PBS by early educators to develop and implement effective behavior support plans for young children with aggression. We offer the story of Cooper as an illustration of how this process works and the outcomes that may be experienced.

The Process for Implementing Positive Behavior Support

Table 1 presents the four steps involved in the process of developing, implementing, and evaluating an effective positive behavior support plan for young children who are engaging in frequent acts of aggression. In the following sections, each step will be described.

Convening a Team

The PBS process begins by convening a team to address the needs of an individual child. The team members should include the classroom teacher, the child's family, and a person who is familiar with PBS that can guide the process (e.g., behavior consultant, mental health consultant, or consulting early childhood special educator). Additional team members may include classroom teaching assistants, therapists, and program administrators. The team gathers to discuss the strengths of the child, their concerns about the behavior the child is displaying, and their goals for the PBS process and child outcomes. The PBS facilitator (i.e., person who will guide the group) describes the steps of the process and enlists the team in deciding how to begin the process.

Conducting a Functional Assessment

The first activity for the team is to conduct the functional assessment. The functional assessment is a process in which a portfolio of observations

Table 1
Process of Positive Behavior Support

Step 1: Convening a team to address needs of individual child
Step 2: Functional assessment
a) Gathering information
b) Developing hypotheses
Step 3: Brainstorm the behavior support plan
Step 4: Implementation, monitor and evaluate the behavior support plan

■▬▬▬▬▬▬▬▬■

Positive Behavior Support (PBS)
offers a promising interven-
tion approach for addressing
aggressive behavior.

and information is gathered and then interpreted (Kern, O'Neill, & Starosta, 2005). Thus, the second step in the process of developing a positive behavior support plan requires the completion of two activities by the team: gathering information and developing a hypothesis (see Table 1). The goal of the functional assessment process is to come to an understanding about how environmental events govern problem behavior. By gathering information on the relationships of contextual triggers and maintaining consequences, the team can begin to draw conclusions about the purpose or function of problem behavior.

The gathering of information phase or the functional assessment portfolio includes many different sources of information. A review of the child's records is performed to gain an understanding of the child's social history, previous placements, developmental assessments, and medical concerns. Second, observations of the child within daily interactions are conducted. These observations occur within activities and situations where problem behavior is likely to occur and not occur. The observations are typically conducted by all of the members of the team. The members of the child's family and teacher may offer observations in the form of notes on incidents of problem behavior that include information on the time of day, situation (setting or interaction), antecedents (what occurred before), and maintaining consequences (what occurred after) that surrounded each incident of aggression.

Finally, most teams use an interview to gather the information that individuals have about the problem behavior, triggers of behavior incidents, consequences that may maintain behavior, and the possible functions (Kern et al., 2005; O'Neill et al., 1997). In conducting the interview, the team first decides who should be able to provide relevant information and then what question to ask. For example, the early educator may provide information on a child's interactions with peers while the parent has information on health concerns or sleeping patterns. An interview is recommended as it provides a relatively efficient way to gather the knowledge of individual team members in a systematic manner.

In addition to reviewing records, direct observation, and interviews, the facilitator of the PBS process may develop other mechanisms for collecting data. For example, if the team suspects that sleep or medication affects problem behavior, then a form for systematically collecting that information in a manner that reveals relationships may be used. That is, if the team suspects that lack of sleep is affecting the child's display of aggression, they would develop a simple data collection system that would provide information on the frequency of aggression and the amount of sleep the child had the previous day.

Once all the information is gathered, the team moves on to developing hypothesis statements about the function of the problem behavior by coming together to synthesize the data (Donnellan, Mirenda, Mesaros, & Fassbender, 1984; Nielsen, Olive, Donovan, & McEvoy, 1998). The data are reviewed to see if there are patterns between triggers of problem behavior, the consequences that follow problem behavior, and the child's response. These data are interpreted through the framework of determining what the child seems to be communicating through the use of problem behavior. The hypotheses typically fall into two categories: the child is trying to obtain something (e.g., activities, sensory stimulation, attention, objects, help) or escape something (e.g., activities, sensory stimulation, attention, objects, help).

Next we describe the functional assessment process that was used to gain an understanding of Cooper's problem behavior.

Once the team was established, a functional assessment was initiated and conducted over a three-week period. The team consisted of Cooper's parents, his two preschool teachers, the preschool director, his speech therapist, and the behavioral consultant. Information was gathered from interviews, direct observations, and archival records, including pediatric and psychological assessments. This information was then synthesized to assist the team in developing hypotheses about the function of Cooper's challenging behavior.

The teaching staff reported that aggressive behavior would occur frequently throughout the school day with the exception of snack and lunch routines. His teachers shared their impressions about Cooper's aggressive behavior. They believed that Cooper appeared to not understand what the expectations were for most of his daily school routines. Staff also reported that if a child was in close proximity and crying loudly, Cooper would approach the child, and immediately attempt to hit, bite, or pinch that child.

All team members expressed concern about Cooper's lack of consistent verbal language, and stated that his deficits in verbal communication may have led Cooper to resort to other forms of interaction, including pointing, whining, crying, or aggression in order to get his needs met. There was concern that Cooper's verbal and receptive deficits may have impacted his ability to learn new skills and communicate in an age-appropriate manner. This severe language delay was seen as being related to his level of aggressive behavior particularly when approaching peers to interact or communicate his needs. The reports of the Part C evaluation, as well as information obtained from his pediatrician and speech therapist, also identified his delayed receptive processing as interfering with Cooper's ability to understand and comprehend verbal instructions and interactions. The team also hypothesized that there was a connection between Cooper's aggressive behavior and the occurrence of specific setting events (i.e., sickness, lack of sleep, exposure to loud noises, or large groups of people in close proximity).

The interviews and assessments confirmed the information gleaned during observations by the behavioral consultant. The team examined the multiple sources of information gathered from the functional assessment and concluded that Cooper's aggressive behavior was more likely to occur during the following circumstances: transitions, high demand activities, changes in routine, nondirected and nonpreferred activities, and tasks associated with unclear expectations. They also identified specific environmental events that served as triggers for Cooper to exhibit aggressive behavior.

The information gathered allowed the team to determine that there were multiple functions maintaining Cooper's aggressive behavior. The team hypothesized Cooper engaged in challenging behavior in an attempt to escape from school activities: (1) that were considered unpredictable or had unclear expectations; (2) that Cooper considered nonpreferred (difficult, boring); (3) that were associated with high levels of noise or people; and (4) in an attempt to gain attention from peer or teacher.

The functional assessment process can be the most difficult and time-consuming step of the PBS process. It is critically important that this step is not overlooked or rushed. The behavior support plan that is developed for the child should be directly linked to the hypothesis statements. If those statements are not developed with integrity to the process, the plan is likely to fail.

Brainstorm the Behavior Support Plan

Once the hypotheses are determined, the team can brainstorm the behavior support plan. It is very important that all members of the team participate in this process, as they are the ones who will be implementing the plan. The behavior support plan should always include four parts: (1) behavior hypothesis statements, (2) specification of prevention strategies, (3) identification of replacement skills, and (4) delineation of new responses to behavior (Bambara & Kern, 2005). We have already described how a behavior hypothesis statement is developed and provided examples of the statements that were developed for Cooper.

The second part of the behavior support plan is the specification of prevention strategies that link directly to the identified triggers for problem behavior. Prevention strategies include modifications in interactions, instructions, environment, activities, materials, and other relevant stimuli that soften the triggers for problem behavior (Kern & Clarke, 2005). These strategies reduce the likelihood that the child would use problem behavior to get his or her needs met.

The next part of the behavior support plan is one of the most important parts, the instruction of replacement skills (Halle, Bambara, & Reichle, 2005). If the team neglects to teach the child new forms of communication that can replace problem behavior, then it is likely that the child will continue to use the problem behavior to communicate wants and needs (Halle et al., 2005). The more quickly the child learns to use these replacement skills, the more quickly the problem behavior will be reduced. Thus, the team needs to ensure that effective and efficient methods of instruction are used to ensure the learning of the targeted replacement skills.

The behavior support plan that is developed for the child should be directly linked to the hypothesis statements.

Replacement skills should be taught to the child throughout the day during the times the child is not having the problem, in addition to opportunities for instruction that occur when the child is redirected. The goal of instruction should be to embed as many trials or opportunities for instruction as possible within the daily routine. Teaching should occur during the time the child is not having problem behavior, as those are times when the child is most receptive to receiving information and guidance from the teacher or peers. Teachers should look for opportunities to embed instruction into routines where the replacement skill may be meaningfully used. For example, if the replacement skill for a child is to tap a peer on the shoulder to initiate peer interaction, the teacher may set up those opportunities throughout the child's day. The child may be prompted to use the new skill during circle time, when passing out materials, when choosing a partner for an art activity, and for requesting a turn with a toy.

In addition to making arrangements to teach the skill throughout the day, the team should determine the method of systematic instruction (or prompting hierarchy) that will be used to teach the skill. There are numerous research-based instructional methods that can be used to ensure that

Table 2
Cooper's Behavior Support Plan

Prevention Strategies	Replacement Skills	Adult Responses
Visual cues/photo schedule/stop signs	Teach how to initiate/terminate interactions	Clear instructions
Social stories	Teach how to initiate appropriate physical affection	Redirect and ignore
First/then boards	Teach how to appropriately ask for "break" or "help"	Specific praise
Choice	Teach how to respond to environmental sensitivities	Provide choice
Preferred items	Teach how to make and express choice	Materials ready
Manipulatives		Consistent verbal cues
Add quiet area		"All done," countdowns
Add breaks		Model
Peer buddy		Encourage verbal interactions
Remove distractions		Monitor and anticipate difficult activities

the skill is efficiently taught (Bailey & Wolery, 1992; Grisham-Brown, Hemmeter, & Pretti-Frontczak, 2005). When instruction is approached haphazardly, many more trials of instruction are needed for skill acquisition and fluency.

Finally, the plan includes new responses to problem behavior and responses to the behaviors that the team wants to be encouraged by adults and peers in the child's natural environments. Problem behavior persists because the child ultimately accesses a reinforcer or gets his needs met. The team must develop a plan to ensure that access to a reinforcer (or maintaining consequence) does not occur while making sure to use strategies that will strengthen the development of desired behaviors and skills. For example, if the child currently uses tantrums to get an adult to come over and help with an object that is difficult to manipulate, then the adult needs to ensure that help is not delivered contingent on problem behavior. An alternate strategy may be to prompt the child to request help (i.e., say "help", gesture "help") before providing help.

Returning to Cooper's team's work, we see the process of developing the support plan and how it is linked to the behavioral hypotheses.

Cooper's support plan includes strategies that are directly related to the escape and attention functions maintaining his aggressive behavior. Table 2 provides a list of prevention strategies identified by Cooper's team that will be used in all routines to help Cooper understand the expectations of the routine, increase the predictability of activities, and alter the desirability of activities. For example, visual cues are provided to increase the level of predictability for each of the routines. That is, representational photos are paired with instructions to help Cooper understand expectations of routines and the sequence of activities. Photos are also placed in strategic areas around the classroom to help cue him about expectations (e.g., where to sit, appropriate behavior). First/then photo boards are also incorporated into daily routines that reflect the sequence of Cooper's day. The photo boards assist with predictability and provide visual prompts for Cooper to increase engagement in nonpreferred activities.

The team also identifies several ways to incorporate choice opportunities, Cooper's preferences, and high-interest materials into his daily routines and activities. Providing choices of activities, preferred items, and interesting materials to Cooper helps change the way he responds to the request for engagement in activities that were previously associated with displays of problem behavior. In addition, the use of choice, preference, and high-interest materials will assist in keeping Cooper engaged in activities for longer periods of time and reduce the display of challenging behavior, allowing his teachers to teach skills and provide positive adult attention. Providing Cooper with choices and preferred objects/activities also helps Cooper cope with events that may have triggered problem behavior in the past. For example, once the plan was in place, Cooper is no longer distracted or aggressive when another child is crying loudly in the classroom. Now, Cooper looks up at his peer momentarily, and then redirects his attention back to a preferred activity (car picture book). Another prevention strategy identified involves the recruitment of a peer buddy to help Cooper play and learn appropriate behavior. The peer buddy and Cooper are provided with high interest toys that will foster the engagement in play. The high-interest items that are shared between the boys provided a way for Cooper to initiate and increase positive social interactions.

A plan is also in place to teach Cooper replacement skills to provide him with an appropriate alternative to aggression. The five priority skills for Cooper to be taught and learn are presented in Table 2. The teaching plan includes having the teachers stop the use of the consequence-based procedure of the "sit-out chair" and concentrating their efforts on identifying naturally occurring conditions to teach Cooper how to respond in a more appropriate manner in order to convey his needs. His team recognizes the importance of teaching replacement skills throughout the day. These replacement skills provide Cooper with alternative ways to interact and respond to others, as well as terminate activities that are difficult, or overwhelming due to environmental sensitivities. For all activities, Cooper will be taught how to initiate appropriately, either verbally or with gestures, to get his needs met. Table 3 provides examples of verbal and nonverbal skills that have been identified by Cooper's team.

The teachers plan to use a variety of instructional strategies for teaching the replacement skills. They plan to attend to specific situations and immediately verbally state what he is attempting to obtain or escape from prior to the occurrence of challenging behavior. This interpretive statement will then be followed by a verbal cue or prompt of the replacement behavior Cooper is expected to display. The teacher will also model the replacement skill, providing Cooper with a clear example of how to display replacement behavior (i.e., "Cooper, you want to play with the cars Harry has. Say, 'I want to share please'").

Table 3
Replacement Skills Taught to Cooper

Skills Taught to Replace Aggressive Behavior	Attention	Escape
Verbal	"I want to share"	"Go away"
	"I need help"	"I want a break"
	"I want a hug/kiss"	"All done"
Nonverbal	Gesture with toy to share	Gesture with STOP sign to end routine/request break
	Gesture for hug/kiss	Point to picture or leave area

Replacement behaviors taught to Cooper will include social interactions, such as how to initiate sharing, asking for a hug, and how to terminate an interaction appropriately. His teachers will teach him the skill of not only how to ask for a hug from other children, but also how to deliver a hug without too much force, or for too long a period of time. Cooper will also be taught how to pat a friend on the arm and pair with a verbal request of "I want a hug please", and then wait for the other child to open his/her arms to receive a hug. Cooper will then hug the peer and stop with a 3-2-1 countdown. This also requires teaching the other children to assist and demonstrate that they are ready to be hugged by opening their arms to Cooper. He will also be taught the skill of asking to play with another's toy. The replacement skills will also allow Cooper to learn how to initiate a break or exit an activity. A laminated 3 x 3 inch representational "stop sign" will be provided to Cooper, and he will be taught to show the stop sign to a teacher and say "All done" when he wants a break or to leave an activity. Once Cooper shows the stop sign or says, "All done", he immediately will be given the opportunity to leave, start another activity, or go to the quiet area in the back of room. The "stop sign" is also effective as a visual redirective prompt when Cooper is having difficulty stopping an activity, such as leaving the bathroom after washing his hands.

Cooper will also be taught a verbal skill to assist with his sensitivities to environmental stimulus by having him learn to request that others leave his immediate area, and communicate that he wants to be alone. For example, if another child is in close proximity and the teacher observes that Cooper is becoming upset, the teacher will state what Cooper wants (e.g., "Cooper you want to be alone, say 'Go away please'"). The other students in the class will also be taught by the teachers to back away from Cooper when he verbalizes this request. In the rare circumstances when this isn't physically possible, he will be given the option to leave and sit in the quiet area. These new skills are designed to empower Cooper with a new and effective way to communicate and get his needs met.

Cooper's team also identified a number of specific ways that they will change their behaviors directed to Cooper. The third column of Table 2 summarizes these. For example, the teachers will modify their delivery of instructions by presenting clear, concise requests to accommodate Cooper's current verbal processing and receptive issues (e.g., "Cooper sit, sit in chair"). Increased specific praise will also be incorporated by the teachers, which will not only increase the positive attention that he receives but also provide feedback about the appropriate behavior exhibited. To reduce distractions and help with predictability, teachers prepare all materials prior to the start of a new activity. Preparing materials allows the teaching staff to have quick access to activity items, and provides a clear and consistent pace of routines, which may help to reduce the aversiveness of various activities for Cooper as well. Teachers will also use a redirect and ignore approach when Cooper becomes aggressive, to reduce the possibility of teachers providing unintended attention to Cooper.

In reviewing Cooper's behavior support plan as presented, the reader can see that each of the four parts have been addressed (i.e., behavior hypothesis statements; specification of prevention strategies; identification of replacement skills; and delineation of new responses to behavior).

Implementation, Monitoring, and Evaluation of the Behavior Support Plan

Once the behavior support plan is developed, the team begins implementation of the plan within daily routines and play. This often involves restructuring activities, providing environmental supports, and changing how adults interact with the child. It is important to develop a written plan in plain language so that all adults understand the actions they need to implement. Often, the behavior consultant will assist the classroom team in the first days of implementation until all members of the team are comfortable with the new procedures.

An outcome monitoring form should be used with plan implementation. It will be important for the team to collect objective data on whether the plan is working and the child is meeting his goals (Janney & Snell, 2000). Behavior support teams may find that the use of simple ratings scales or checklists that are individually designed to track one or two of the desired outcomes will be the easiest form of data collection to implement in a busy classroom. For example, a teacher may count the number of times the child has a tantrum during circle time and look for those incidents to decrease paired with noting the amount of time the child is actively engaged in circle time activities. In the home setting, a family may be provided with a rating scale to summarize the child's affective state (e.g., 1= smiling and cooperative, 2= some problem behaviors, or 3= crying and resistive) during a target routine.

Summary

Positive Behavior Support provides an effective approach for developing individualized behavior support plans that result in important outcomes for children, their teachers, and families. While the process may be complex and require the guidance of a behavior consultant who is knowledgeable about the process, there is a growing body of information and

Figure 1
Total Number of Aggressions Occurring Daily During First 15 Minutes of Targeted Routines

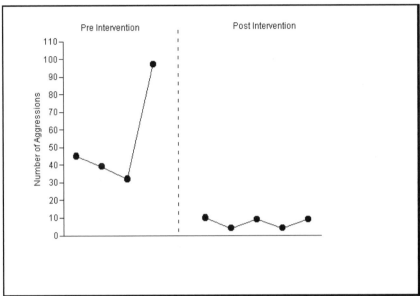

materials specific to early childhood applications of this model (see www. csefel.uiuc.edu or www.challengingbehavior.org for more information). This approach was pivotal in the support of Cooper and his successful inclusion in preschool. In closing, we describe the outcomes that Cooper and his team experienced.

The intervention strategies and replacement skills incorporated into Cooper's daily preschool activities substantially improved his behavioral repertoire and reduced his aggressive behavior. In an effort to examine change in behavior over time, a frequency count of the number of aggressive acts Cooper displayed across five days was recorded. Because his rates of aggression were so high, the teachers decided to count the number of aggressions that occurred within the first 15 minutes of targeted activities. Figure 1 shows the total number of aggressions that occurred during free play, circle, centers, art, and outdoor play. Once intervention was implemented, the number was compared with the five days following intervention implementation and the reduction was substantial. In addition to the reduction in aggression following intervention, Cooper's teachers and parents noticed that he had become much happier in the classroom and at home. Team members reported that Cooper was smiling, jumping, clapping, and dancing in his classroom and at home much more fol-

lowing the introduction of the behavior support plan. Following the implementation of the plan, Cooper was spontaneously using the verbal requests, gestures, and physical affection skills taught not only during the school day, but also at his home. His new replacement skills enabled Cooper to request or terminate interaction and/or activities either verbally or nonverbally, in a manner that was easily interpreted by other children in the classroom. His parents also noted that Cooper started verbalizing much more with his family, requesting preferred toys, choosing and expressing his preference for snack, as well as asking to go outside, where he previously ran out of his house without permission. There was also a notable change in his relationships with his classmates, and the way the other children in the classroom interacted and responded to Cooper.

As a result of this behavior reduction and the ongoing effectiveness of the comprehensive support plan, it was decided by the team that Cooper should be allowed to continue his attendance at preschool and the threat of expulsion was removed. In addition, his parents and teachers felt he was now capable of attending the preschool for the entire school day. With the ongoing implementation of the behavior support plan in all daily routines, Cooper adjusted well to the change in the length of his preschool day. His teachers reported that following his full-time attendance over four weeks, Cooper was no longer exhibiting aggressive behavior. His teachers were pleased to report that Cooper was doing well in preschool and that he often would assume roles as a "leader and teacher's helper."

Notes

Development of this article was supported in part by funding from the U.S. Department of Education, Office of Special Education Programs grant: H324D020040. The opinions and other content contained in this article do not necessarily reflect the opinion of the agency, and no official endorsement should be inferred. The authors would like to acknowledge and thank Cooper and his family for their participation in this case study and recognize the efforts of the preschool staff and other members of the PBS team. Lise Fox can be reached by e-mail at fox@fmhi.usf.edu

References

Bailey, D. & Wolery, M. (1992). *Teaching infants and preschoolers with disabilities*. New York: Macmillan.

Bambara, L. M. & Kern, L. (2005). *Individualized supports for students with problem behaviors*. New York: Guilford Press.

Campbell, S. B. (1995). Behavior problems in preschool children: A review of recent research. *Journal of Child Psychology and Psychiatry, 36*(1), 113-149.

Carr, E. G., Horner, R. H., Turnbull, A. P., Marquis, J. G., Magito-McLaughlin, D., & McAtee, M. L. et al. (1999). *Positive behavior support as an approach for dealing with problem behavior in people with developmental disabilities: A research synthesis*. Washington, DC: AAMR.

Coie, J. D. & Dodge, K. A. (1998). Aggression and antisocial behavior. In N. Eisenberg (Ed.), *Handbook of child psychology: Vol. 3, Social, emotional, and personality development* (5th ed., pp. 779-862). New York: Wiley.

Conroy, M. A., Dunlap, G., Clarke, S., & Alter, P. (2005). A descriptive analysis of positive behavioral intervention research with young children with challenging behavior. *Topics in Early Childhood Special Education, 25*, 157-166.

della Cava, M. (2005, September 20). Out-of-line preschoolers increasingly face expulsion. *USA TODAY*, p. N1.

Dishion, T. J., French, D. C., & Patterson, G. R. (1995). The development and ecology of antisocial behavior. In D. Cicchetti & D. J. Cohen (Eds.), *Developmental psychopathology, Vol. 2: Risk, disorder, and adaptation* (pp. 421-471). New York: John Wiley & Sons.

Dobbs, M. (2005, May 17). Youngest students most likely to be expelled. *The Washington Post*, p. A02.

Donnellan, A. M., Mirenda, P. L., Mesaros, R. A., & Fassbender, L. L. (1984). Analyzing the communicative functions of aberrant behavior. *Journal of the Association for Persons with Severe Handicaps, 9*, 201-212.

Egeland, B., Kalkoske, M., Gottesman, N., & Erickson, M. F. (1990). Preschool behavior problems: Stability and factors accounting for change. *Journal of Child Psychology and Psychiatry, 31*, 891-909.

Fox, L., Dunlap, G., & Cushing, L. (2002). Early intervention, positive behavior support, and transition to school. *Journal of Emotional and Behavior Disorders, 10*(3), 149-157.

Fox, L., Dunlap, G., & Powell, D. (2002). Young children and challenging behavior: Issues and considerations for behavior support. *Journal of Positive Behavior Interventions, 4*, 208-217.

Grisham-Brown, J., Hemmeter, M. L., & Pretti-Frontczak, K. (2005). *Blended practices for teaching young children in inclusive settings*. Baltimore: Paul H. Brookes.

Halle, J., Bambara, L. M., & Reichle, J. (2005). Teaching alternative skills. In L. M. Bambara & L. Kern (Eds.), *Individualized supports for students with problem behaviors* (pp. 129-164). New York: Guilford Press.

Janney, R. & Snell, M. E. (2000). *Behavioral support*. Baltimore: Paul H. Brookes.

Kern, L. & Clarke, S. (2005). Antecedent and setting event interventions. In L. M. Bambara & L. Kern (Eds.), *Individualized supports for students with problem behaviors* (pp. 201-236). New York: Guilford Press.

Kern, L., O'Neill, R. R., & Starosta, K. (2005). Gathering functional assessment information. In L. M. Bambara & L. Kern (Eds.), *Individualized supports for students with problem behaviors* (pp. 129-164). New York: Guilford Press.

Lewin, T. (2005, May 17). Research finds a high rate of expulsions in preschool. *The New York Times*, p E1.

Nielsen, S. L, Olive, M. L., Donovan, A., & McEvoy, M. (1998). Challenging behaviors in your classroom? Don't react – Teach instead. *Young Exceptional Children, 2*(1), 2-10.

O'Neill, R. E., Horner, R. H., Albin, R.W., Storey, K., Sprague, J.R., & Newton, J.S. (1997). *Functional Assessment of problem behavior: A practical assessment guide*. Pacific Grove, CA: Brookes/Cole.

Pierce, E. W., Ewing, L. J., & Campbell, S. B. (1999). Diagnostic status and symptomatic behavior of hard-to-manage preschool children in middle childhood and early adolescence. *Journal of Clinical Child Psychology, 28*, 44-57.

Reid, J. B. (1993). Prevention of conduct disorder before and after school entry: Relating interventions to developmental findings. *Development and Psychopathology, 5*, 243-262.

You Got To Have Friends

Promoting Friendships for Preschool Children

Phillip S. Strain, Ph.D.,
University of Colorado at Denver

Gail E. Joseph, Ph.D.,
University of Denver

Cesar is one of the more popular children in his preschool class. He often joins his classmates in creating unusual and fun imaginary games. He readily shares toys and materials, often proposing a trade that works for all. Cesar laughs a lot; he is enthusiastic, and he almost always says, "Yes" when a classmate asks him to play or has a different play idea. Cesar also says nice things to his classmates and acknowledges their accomplishments. When it is time to choose a friend for an activity Cesar is always in great demand.

Chloe is one of Cesar's classmates. She spends most of her time in preschool staying close to her teacher, occasionally hovering around a group of children playing together. Chloe doesn't say much to her classmates and they in turn seldom speak to her. Chloe, in fact, has lots of skills. She knows what to do with toys and utensils; she knows the usual "scripts" that emerge in imaginary play. Chloe, however, seldom gets chosen by another classmate to participate together. In her world of social isolation she occasionally appears sad to the outside observer.

The behavioral contrast between Cesar and Chloe is profound. Cesar has classmates who advocate for him, encourage him, and include him. Chloe, on the other hand, is like an invisible member of the class. No one asks, "Where's Chloe," no one says, "We need Chloe," no one says, "Come on Chloe!" The differing social worlds experienced by Chloe and Cesar not only predict very divergent developmental trajectories in preschool, but they set the occasion for lifelong consequences. Based upon longitudinal and retrospective research (Hartup & Moore, 1990; Howes, 1990; Kupersmidt, Coie, & Dodge, 1990), it is clear that Cesar is on a developmental path toward self-confidence, continual friendships, school success, and healthy adult adjustment. Chloe is sadly on a developmental path toward deepening isolation, loneliness, and adult mental health problems. Early friendships have been identified as the most powerful single predictor of long-term social adjustment (Strain & Schwartz, 2001).

What Behaviors Lead to Friendship?

A number of discrete behaviors that young children engage in during play with each other have been found to be directly related to these children having friends (Tremblay, Strain, Hendrickson, & Shores, 1981). That is, children who do more of these behaviors are more likely to have friends. The specific behaviors identified by Tremblay and colleagues include: (1) Organizing Play—with preschoolers, these are usually "Let's" statements, such as, "Let's play trucks." Often these "Let's" statements are followed by suggestions about roles (e.g., "You be the driver") or specific activities (e.g., "Roll it to me"); (2) Sharing—takes many forms among preschoolers. Children with friends request in the form of "Can I have some paint" and they also oblige share requests from peers. (3) Assisting Others—this also takes many forms at the preschool level. Children can help each other onto or off of an apparatus, tell or show a friend how to do something, or assist someone in distress. (4) Giving compliments—these behaviors do not often occur among preschoolers, but they tend to have a powerful effect on the formation of friendships. Preschoolers compliment one another's successes, play accomplishments (e.g., block buildings, artwork, playground feats), and appearance (e.g., clothing, shoes, jewelry, hair).

In addition to engaging in these discrete behaviors, the formation of friendship is equally dependent upon two patterns of interaction. First, it is necessary for children to be reciprocal in their interactions (Guralnick, 1990; Tremblay et al., 1981). Reciprocity has two dimensions. Initially, children need to be responsive to the social bids of others. Also, over a period of time (i.e., several months), it is important that there be a relatively equal number of occasions that each member of a friendship dyad starts an interaction. In addition to reciprocity, the length of interaction occurrences also characterizes friendship patterns of interaction. That is, friendship pairs engage in more lengthy episodes.

In the following sections, we describe a series of strategies that teachers can use to promote children's friendships. Specifically, we highlight setting the stage for play and strategies for developing friendships (i.e., instructional strategies and strategies for supporting practice opportunities).

Setting the Stage for Friendship

Prior to beginning instruction in friendly behavior, teachers need to attend to five elements of the classroom. First, an inclusive classroom where children with disabilities are meaningfully included in natural proportions is critical to setting the stage (Guralnick, 1990). Second, the presence and pre-selection of cooperative-use toys and materials increase the opportunities for social interaction (Hendrickson, Strain, Tremblay, & Shores, 1982; Ivory & McCollum, 1999). Cooperative-use toys are those that naturally lend themselves to two or more children playing together. For example, materials such as balls, puppets, wagons, teeter-totters, dress-up clothes, and board games require that young children coordinate their play. Third, it is necessary to examine all classroom routines and embed social interaction instruction and practice opportunities throughout the day (Brown & Odom, 1994; McEvoy, Fox, & Rosenberg, 1991). Table 1 provides an example of how one teacher decided to embed social interaction practice opportunities into her classroom routines. Fourth, in order to ensure that social interaction instruction and practice opportunities have the necessary importance, teachers need to include social interaction goals and/or outcomes on a child's IEP/IFSP. While social competence outcomes are likely to be some of the most critical for the child's later development, they often do not appear on IEPs or IFSPs (McConnell, McEvoy, & Odom, 1992). Fifth, and likely most importantly, teachers need to devote energy toward creating a classroom climate with an ethos of friendship (Fox, Dunlap, Hemmeter, Joseph, & Strain, & 2003). When one walks into a classroom where a teacher has done this successfully, you see adults give time and attention to children when they engage in friendly behaviors, you hear adults talk nicely to one another, you hear children supporting one another's friendly behavior. Overall, you get a sense that friendship is the ultimate goal.

Strategies for Developing Friendships

Setting the stage is a necessary element of supporting children's developing friendships. However, some children will require systematic teaching in order to develop the skills that lead to having friends (Strain & Schwartz, 2001). This teaching involves implementing instructional activities addressing appropriate behavior as well as adult and peer strategies that provide for practice opportunities with feedback.

Table 1
Example of Schedule With Embedded Friendship Opportunities

Arrival	Find a "buddy" to walk with from the bus to class. One child is the "greeter" and greets children by name as they arrive.
Circle Time	One child is selected to pass out the circle time props to each classmate. As the child progresses around the circle they call each child by their name and say, "pick a ___." Each child then responds with, "Thanks (child's name)." After children have a chance to use the circle time prop they will trade with a friend. Children identify a "buddy" to play with at choice time. The pair must decide together where they will play first.
Free Choice	Children will play with their "buddy" (assigned or selected) for the first ten minutes of free choice time. If they stick with their buddy the whole time they get special reward (e.g., sticker, stamp on hand). Adults watch for friendly behaviors and provide reinforcement Set up the "buddy" table. Children must find a friend to play at the table with in order to gain access to the high preference toys there.
Small Group	Plan cooperative art projects: "Buddy Art" Teach children to play board games (e.g., "Barnyard Bingo," "Candy Land," "Don't spill the beans"). Put children in charge of different materials needed for the small group project (e.g., Tommy has the glue, Helen has the sequins, Haley has the paper, etc.). The children must use their peer's name to request materials. Adults reinforce children for sharing.
Outside	Pre-select cooperative use toys for outside play (e.g., tire swings, wagons, double tricycles, balls). Adults organize peer play (e.g., Duck, Duck, Goose; Red Rover; Farmer in the Dell; tag). Adults watch for and reinforce friendly behavior at appropriate times.

Implementing Instructional Activities

An approach referred to as "role-play modeling" has been recommended as an effective method for providing instructions in skills that lead to having friends and can include adults, peers, or even puppets demonstrating the friendship skill, or video-based modeling with short vignettes of children engaging in friendly behavior (Webster-Stratton & Hammond, 1997). The use of both examples and non-examples followed by opportunities for correct responding are recommended when implementing a role-play modeling intervention.

Table 1 (*continued*)

Snack	Have each child in charge of different snack items (e.g., Joey has juice, Haley has crackers, Sam has orange slices, Ben has cups). Children have to ask each other for the snack items from a peer. Adults reinforce children for sharing.
Story time	Select books with friendship themes. Children share a larger carpet square with a friend.
Goodbye circle	Compliment circle – children have a chance to give a friend a compliment while passing around the "compliment bear." One child can pass out backpacks from the cubbies as children leave. One child can say goodbye to each classmate.
Transitions	During choice time, instead of transitioning to a center – transition to a friend (use a friend picture schedule). Children can hold hands going from one activity to another. One child can give children a high-five as they come in from outside. During clean-up, adults reinforce children's helping behavior.

We have identified four guiding principles of effective role-play modeling strategies. The first guiding principle of modeling is to use invisible support, that is, call on the child who you are confident will model the skill appropriately before calling on a child who will need more support. Second, sometimes when children are modeling the friendship skill in front of their peers, they can get carried away with being silly or inappropriate. It is important to give the child another chance and support so that they are successful in demonstrating the skill positively. This opportunity allows them to receive positive reinforcement from the teacher for doing the skill. Third, because role plays typically involve only one or two children at a time, it is necessary to plan ways for the rest of the children to be engaged actively. This involvement can include giving a thumbs up for friendly behavior and a thumbs down for unfriendly; patting themselves on the back if this is a behavior they do; clapping when the role play is over; saying "ready, set, action" before the role play begins; or having a popsicle stick sign with a happy face on one side and a sad face on the other (children show the happy face when the behavior being modeled is friendly and the sad face when the behavior being modeled is unfriendly). The final principle addresses the issue of ensuring equal opportunities for all children. That is, it is important to keep track of who has had a chance to role play and ensure that all of the children in the class get a turn sometime during the week.

As noted earlier, a strategy for implementing role-play modeling that is sometimes used and has been shown to be effective is the use of video vignettes (Webster-Stratton & Hammond, 1997). Video-based modeling is particularly effective for several reasons. First, videos can capture pristine examples of children using friendly behavior. These examples can be used to generate discussion about the friendly behavior, and the context in which it is used on the video. Also, these examples can be used as a standard with which to compare the children's practice attempts. Video vignettes can also display non-examples. These vignettes can be used to teach children to discriminate between friendly and unfriendly behavior and prompt children to develop and share alternative behaviors and solutions if initial ideas are not effective. Second, video clips can be frozen (i.e., paused) and children can be prompted to attend to the often-fleeting salient features of the friendly behaviors and the context in which they occur. Children can also make predictions about "what will happen next" when the child featured in the video uses a friendly or unfriendly behavior. Third, the very format of video is particularly powerful in engaging and keeping children's attention.

Similar to video vignettes, puppets have also been used as an effective strategy for engaging young children in the modeling of friendship skills (Webster-Stratton & Hammond, 1997). Since the play of preschool children often involves fantasy, puppets, in essence, join children in this fantasy world while modeling positive friendship skills. Because adults are in control of the puppet, the puppet can always be a responsive play partner. The puppet can model friendly play, and when appropriate and planned, can model non-examples. Puppets in the image of children are particularly effective because they provide a proximate model. That is, children are more likely to emulate the behavior of models that look like themselves. Additionally, some children will disclose more about their feelings and friendship problems to puppets than to adults, especially if adults are historically not seen as trustworthy by the child (Wusterbarth & Strain, 1980).

Supporting Practice Opportunities

As noted earlier, in addition to developing specific activities for systematically teaching skills that lead to having friends, teachers must also identify opportunities throughout the routines and activities of the day (as illustrated in Table 1). However, in order to make the most of these embedded learning opportunities, teachers must systematically embed teaching and support strategies (Horn, Lieber, Schwartz, & Sandall, 2000). These teaching and support strategies should include both peer and adult behaviors.

Peer Support Strategies. When typical children are assisting their classmates with special needs to acquire friendship skills, it is necessary for them to learn to suspend social rules in order not to feel rejected (Strain, 2001). In the usual course of events, interactions between typical children are usually quite reciprocal. If someone asks nicely to play, they usually get a positive response. On the other hand, as children with special needs begin to acquire peer interaction skills, they often reject the social overtures of their peers and seldom initiate play. Using role-play and rehearsal strategies, there is a well-researched set of procedures for teaching typical peers to be persistent with their social behavior while their peers with special needs are becoming more fluent (Strain, 2001). Simply put, adults model peer rejection, provide verbal feedback ("That's what might happen when you ask kids to play") and then provide a behavioral alternative that they reinforce ("if that happens, try again" —"good, you tried again.").

The use of a "buddy system" when trying to increase the friendship skills of children has also been shown to be an effective strategy (Odom & Brown, 1993). In this approach, right before a free-play period children are assigned to a buddy role, meaning that they begin freeplay in some planned play activity with a certain child. In utilizing a buddy system there are several rules to follow. First, it is important to always have two or more buddies for each child with special needs. This arrangement helps to keep the play interesting for the socially competent children and it helps to create conditions for maximizing the number of diverse play ideas. Second, it is important to rotate buddies for several reasons. First, rotating buddies helps to ensure that children have the opportunity to engage in friendship skills with the widest variety of playmates. Second, rotating helps to avoid "buddy-burnout," a condition in which children come to respond negatively to their helper role because they always play with the same individual. Third, one can optimize the buddy system by pairing the most popular and liked children with those that need the most help. This type of pairing can lead to other children simultaneously helping their peers because the "cool" kids are doing it. Finally, at the end of a play period children should receive specific praise for being buddies – praise that specifically enumerates the friendly ways they interacted with their assigned partner.

Adult Teaching and Support Strategies. Through the use of a variety of teaching behaviors, teachers can increase the likelihood that children will learn and use skills that lead to making friends. These teaching behaviors include priming, suggesting play ideas, providing a direct model, and the provision of reinforcement of appropriate behaviors.

Teachers can increase the likelihood of children using friendship skills with specific priming strategies. For example, prior to a free-play period teachers can ask children who they are going to play with or what specific toy or material they are going to share, and they can provide practice opportunities. A practice opportunity might include, "Hey Josh, let's pretend I am Cody and you are going to ask me to play trucks." Josh would then practice asking, with or without adult prompting, and the adult would provide reinforcement or corrective feedback for Josh's social initiation to play.

Teachers can increase the duration of peer play by providing suggestions or prompting role reversals (Bovey & Strain, 2003). Expanding play ideas can occur by suggesting new ways of playing with the materials, for dramatic play to unfold, and including more children in a game or activity. When a teacher notices children are disengaging from play with one another, he or she can prompt the children to reverse dramatic play roles ("how about you be the mom now and she is the baby?"). This can reengage children in the play sequence and lead to more lengthy social encounters.

Another way to keep children engaged in friendly play is to directly model desired behaviors as a play partner. When teachers notice that children are becoming less engaged they can join the playgroup and provide specific models of friendly behavior. For example, a teacher might join two children who are playing together and begin to share the materials available.

While it is almost always necessary to reinforce children for their emerging friendly behavior, it is also the case that the proper use of reinforcement requires ongoing attention to several key factors. First, timing of reinforcement delivery is crucial. As long as children are engaged in friendly behavior, it is a good idea to withhold reinforcement. While this may seem counterintuitive, evidence suggests that adults' delivery of attention to children at play can have the immediate effect of terminating their play (Timm, Strain, & Eller, 1979). Given this fact, it is more advisable to comment on children's friendly play shortly after the fact. When commenting on children's friendly play, it is essential to describe the specific friendly behavior(s) that you observed. Instead of saying, "you're playing so nicely together" say, "you are taking turns and saying nice things to each other." This descriptive commenting provides children with specific feedback about what they are doing well. For many children, teachers may need to provide lots of reinforcement early on. Once children start to use their friendly behaviors, however, teachers need to begin the process of slowly removing their specific feedback from the ongoing play. The goal is not to remove all teacher reinforcement, but to provide sufficient opportunity for friendly play in and of itself to become reinforcing.

Conclusion

Several thousand years ago, Aristotle suggested about friendship, "Who would choose to live, even if possessed with all other things, without friends." Based upon what is now known from longitudinal studies, it is clear that Aristotle was on the right track (Asher & Renshaw, 1981; Shonkoff & Phillips, 2000). It is also the case that the vast majority of children with special needs do not develop friendship skills without thoughtful instruction. In this paper we have highlighted the specific skills known to influence friendship at the preschool level. These skills and patterns of behavior may be considered as the scope of instruction most likely to lead to friendship. We also describe a variety of strategies for creating a classroom climate conducive to friendship development. Finally, we describe specific empirically validated strategies for teaching friendship skills.

One of the struggles that all teachers face is how best to allocate their always limited, always stretched resources. We hope that this paper successfully communicates the fundamental importance of friendship skills along with a straightforward set of strategies to maximize children's opportunities to live in a social world where "everyone knows their name."

Note
You can reach Phillip Strain by e-mail at phil.strain@cudenver.edu

References
Asher, S. R. & Renshaw, P. D. (1981). Children without friends. In S. Asher & J. Gottman, (Eds.), *The development of children's friendships* (pp. 273-296). New York: Cambridge Press.
Bovey, E. H. & Strain, P. S. (2003). *Promoting positive peer social interactions*. Center on the Social and Emotional Foundations for Early Learning: What Works Brief. Retrieved on June 14, 2006 from http://www.csefel.uiuc.edu
Brown, W. H. & Odom, S. L. (1994). Strategies and tactics for promoting generalization and maintenance of young children's social behavior. *Research in Developmental Disabilities*, 15(2), 99-118.
Fox, L., Dunlap, G., Hemmeter, M. L.; Joseph, G. E., & Strain, P. S. (2003). The Teaching Pyramid: A Model for Supporting Social Competence and Preventing Challenging Behavior in Young Children. *Young Children*, 58(4), 48-52.
Guralnick, M. J. (1990). Social competence and early intervention. *Journal of Early Intervention*, 14, 3-14.
Hartup, W. W. & Moore, S. G. (1990). Early peer relations: Developmental significance and prognostic implications. *Early Childhood Research Journal*, 5, 1-17.
Hendrickson, J. M., Strain, P. S., Tremblay, A., & Shores, R. E. (1982). Relationship between toy and material use and the occurrence of social interactive behaviors by normally developing preschool children. *Psychology in the Schools*, 19, 212-220.
Horn, E. M., Lieber, J., Schwartz, I., & Sandall, S. (2000) Supporting young children's IEPs in inclusive settings through embedded learning opportunities. *Topics in Early Childhood Special Education*, 20(4), 208-223.
Howes, C. (1990). Social status of friendship from kindergarten to third grade. *Journal of Applied Developmental Psychology*, 11, 324-330.
Ivory, J. J. & McCollum, J. A. (1999). Effects of social and isolate toys on social play in an inclusive setting. *Journal of Special Education*, 32(4), 238-243.

Kupersmidt, J. B., Coie, J. D., & Dodge, K. A. (1990). The role of poor peer relationships in the development of disorder. In S. Asher & J. Coie (Eds.), *Peer Rejection in Childcare* (pp.274-305). New York: Cambridge University Press.

McConnell, S. R., McEvoy, M. A., & Odom, S. L. (1992). Implementation of social competence interventions in early childhood special education classes: current practices and future directions. In S. L. Odom, S. R. McConnell, & M. A. McEvoy (Eds.), *Social competence of young children with disabilities* (pp. 277-306). Baltimore: Brookes.

McEvoy, M. A., Fox, J. J., & Rosenberg, M. S. (1991). Organizing preschool environments: Suggestions for enhancing the development/learning of preschool children with handicaps. *Topics in Early Childhood Special Education*, 11(2), 18-28.

Odom, S. L. & Brown, W. H. (1993). Social interaction skills interventions for young children with disabilities in integrated settings. In C. A. Peck, S. L. Odom, & D. D. Bricker (Eds.), Integrating young children with disabilities into community programs. Baltimore: Brookes.

Shonkoff, J. P. & Phillips, D. A., (Eds.) (2000). *From neurons to neighborhoods: The science of early childhood development*. Washington, DC: National Academy Press.

Strain, P. S. (2001). Empirically-based social skill intervention. *Behavioral Disorders*, 27, 30-36.

Strain, P. S. & Schwartz, I. (2001). Applied behavior analysis and social skills intervention for young children with autism. *Focus on Autism and Other Developmental Disorders*, 8, 12-24.

Timm, M. A., Strain, P. S., & Eller, P. H. (1979). Effects of systematic, response-dependent fading and thinning procedures on the maintenance of child-child interaction. *Journal of Applied Behavior Analysis*, 12, 308.

Tremblay, A., Strain, P. S., Hendrickson, J. M., & Shores, R. E. (1981). Social interactions of normally developing preschool children: Using normative data for subject and target behavior selection. *Behavior Modification*, 5, 237-253.

Webster-Stratton, C. & Hammond, M. (1997). Treating children with early onset conduct problems: A comparison of child and parent training interventions. *Journal of Consulting and Clinical Psychology*, 65(1), 93-109.

Wusterbarth, N. J. & Strain, P. S. (1980). Effects of adult-mediated attention on the social behavior of physically-abused and neglected preschool children. *Education and Treatment of Children*, 3, 91-99.

Using Assessment to Guide Social-Emotional Intervention for Very Young Children

An Individual Growth and Development Indicator (IGDI) of Parent-Child Interaction

Kathleen M. Baggett, Ph.D.,
University of Kansas

Judith J. Carta, Ph.D.,
University of Kansas

As a home visitor for an Early Head Start program, Jodi visits infants and toddlers and their families each week. She understands that parent-child interactions play an important role in the development of social-emotional competencies in early childhood. These early interactions set the stage for positive social-emotional behavior and development, either through warm, responsive scaffolding that supports the emergence of new social-emotional skills or through non-responsive behaviors that fail to support or directly interfere with competency development and that can lead to social-emotional problems (Landry, Smith, & Swank, in press). Consequently, one of the most important charges of early intervention is to help children establish social-emotional competencies by supporting their parents and primary caregivers in providing the critical ingredients for fostering positive social-emotional behaviors. In a review of 17 home-based early intervention programs, one of the most highly rated outcome goals was the promotion of sensitive parenting behavior (Brooks-Gunn, Berlin, Fuligni, & Sidle, 2000).

The goal of the Early Head Start program in which Jodi works is to promote children's development through parent support. While the program is charged with improving child outcomes across all developmental domains, there is special recognition of the need for monitoring and improving social-emotional outcomes. She often wonders about the social-emotional functioning of children on her caseload,

*especially with families who are repeatedly experiencing high levels
of stress and crises. She wants to be sure that she is providing opportunities for parents to better understand their children's social-emotional needs and to respond in ways that promote children's positive
social-emotional behavior. In particular, she would really like to be
able to identify risky parent-child interactions so that she knows when
to intensify or implement a new intervention. Jodi's program director
would also like to have some way of identifying when intervention is
working so that program outcomes can be shown. Both Jodi and the
program director agree that to do this, Jodi would need a tool that is
easy to learn how to use and that could be completed very quickly
during busy home visits.*

As with many early intervention programs, the program in the vignette
conducts occasional assessments at
the beginning and end of the year.
These measures provide little information to help her make decisions about
intervention. While there are a variety
of measures for assessing infants and
toddlers, practitioners who work with
very young children and their families
have few options when it comes to tools
that they can use on a regular basis to
guide intervention (Carta et al., 2002).
To date, the field of early intervention

*One of the most important
charges of early intervention
is to help children establish
social-emotional competencies
by supporting their parents and
primary caregivers in providing the critical ingredients for
fostering positive social-emotional behaviors.*

has focused more attention on assessment for documenting a delay or
diagnosis as compared to assessment designed to inform intervention
decision-making (Meisels & Atkins-Burnett, 2001). Consequently, there is
a gap between available measures and the tools needed by practitioners
such as Jodi, whose efforts focus on improving outcomes for young children (Carta et al., 2002). This gap is illustrated by a host of limitations
of more commonly available measures, which include administration
requirements beyond the training and experience of most early intervention service providers, measures that are too long and complicated for
repeated use in authentic environments such as homes and child care settings, and lack of readily available reports that can show progress toward
important outcomes.

A recent advance in early childhood assessment is the General Outcome
Measurement (GOM) approach. While this approach has been used for
many years with older children, it is relatively new for use with very young
children (Greenwood, Carta, & Walker, 2005). This approach provides an

alternative to traditional assessment approaches, such as criterion-referenced approaches that do not lend themselves to frequently monitoring growth and development over time (McConnell, Priest, Davis, & McEvoy, 2001). Specifically, GOM approaches contribute to data-based decision-making about intervention by highlighting discrepancies between current levels of functioning and expected levels of functioning by measuring the same set of key skills over time. This is done for the purpose of implementing intervention or modifying intervention to reduce the discrepancy (Deno, 1997).

Individual Growth and Development Indicators (IGDIs) are an example of a GOM approach. They measure key indicators of functioning in a particular domain that have been associated with important general outcomes. Such measures have long been used in pediatric settings. For example, height and weight charts are used to monitor children's growth over time, and taking a temperature serves as a quick indicator of illness that is used repeatedly to monitor progress toward health. These examples share several commonalities: they are brief, easy to administer, designed to be used repeatedly over time for the express purpose of monitoring growth or change, and provide practitioners with immediate feedback to guide intervention decisions. Within the past several years, IGDIs have begun to emerge in the field of early intervention to monitor progress toward meaningful general outcomes, such as communication, problem-solving, and social skills (Carta, Greenwood, Luze, Cline, & Kuntz, 2004; Greenwood et al., 2005).

Illustration of a Parent-Child Interaction IGDI for Infants and Toddlers

The Indicator of Parent-Child Interaction (IPCI) is an Individual Growth and Development Indicator. The IPCI is a means of checking growth toward the important general outcome of interactions in which parents and other primary caregivers respond to their child in ways that promote positive social-emotional behaviors. This general outcome is directly related to social-emotional competence, another highly accepted and valued general outcome in early childhood. Performance is measured through repeated assessment of the same key skills using the same set of care-giving activities and scoring procedure. Change is determined by graphing performance as rate of progress over time (McConnell et al., 2001).

Unique features of the IPCI as compared to common limitations of many existing approaches include the following: (1) focus is on key parent and child behaviors that signal or indicate quality of parent-child interaction and that are predictive of social-emotional outcomes in young children; (2) focus is on activities that typically occur in authentic environments where parents/caregivers and very young children interact; (3) it can be administered by a variety of practitioners that typically provide early intervention services (e.g., early intervention teachers, family support advocates, parent aides, nurses, social workers); (4) it is designed for quick and frequently repeated administration in family homes or center-based settings; and (5) reports can be generated automatically to guide intervention decision-making.

The IPCI is a means of checking growth toward the important general outcome of interactions in which parents and other primary caregivers respond to their child in ways that promote positive social-emotional behaviors.

Content

The IPCI is comprised of a total of 14 items that span competency and difficulty domains for both parents or other caregivers and children. For the parent competency domain, items reflect responsive behaviors that are associated with and have been shown to support or facilitate more positive child social-emotional outcomes (see Landry, Smith, Swank, Assel, & Vallet, 2001; Landry et al., in press; van den Boom, 1994, 1995). Hence, the competency domain for parents is called "Facilitators" and is comprised of five key elements, which include acceptance/warmth, descriptive language, following child's lead, introducing/extending child's interest, and stress-reducing strategies. For example, stress-reducing strategies occur when a parent gives a brief break from interaction when a child shows signals of frustration or a parent swaddles or provides a pacifier to comfort a young infant who is crying frantically at the end of a dressing routine.

The parent difficulty domain consists of behaviors that interrupt interaction and have been associated with poorer child outcomes (see Appleyard, Egeland, van Dulmen, & Sroufe, 2005; Chang, Schwartz, Dodge, & McBride-Chang, 2003). This domain is called "Interrupters" and includes three key elements: Critical Comments/Voice Tone, Restrictions/Intrusions, and Rejecting Child Bids for Support. Examples of Restrictions/Intrusions include both verbal and nonverbal prohibitions, such as a parent pulling a large, clean, and safe ring toy out of an infant's hand or mouth during free-play.

For children, the competency domain pertains to Engagement and is comprised of Positive Feedback, Sustained Engagement, and Follow-through. An example of child Follow-through would be observed during a Dressing routine in which a parent smiles, holds open a shirt sleeve, and says 'Put your hand through this hole' and the child raises her hand toward the open shirt sleeve. The difficulty domain, Distress, includes Overwhelmed by Negative Affect; Externalizing Behaviors, such as tantrums; and Internalizing Behaviors, such as withdrawing from interaction. An example of Internalizing Behavior is a young toddler who during free-play flinches when a parent raises her hand, pulls away from the parent, and who withdraws from interaction while watching the parent from a distance with wide-open eyes. When problems within these domains emerge for young children, they tend to be durable over time without intervention and to be associated with later social-emotional and behavioral problems that can interfere with school readiness (Bricker, Schoen Davis, & Squires, 2004; Briggs-Gowan, Carter, Irwin, Wachtel, & Cicchetti, 2004; Raver, 2003).

Administration

The Indicator of Parent-Child Interaction is completed following a series of brief interaction episodes between a parent and their young child at home or between a familiar caregiver and a child in center-based program during a 10-minute observation period. For children who are older than 1 year, activities include (1) free-play, (2) book reading, (3) a distraction task, and (4) a routine dressing task. For children who are one year old or younger, activities are the same as for older children, excluding the distraction task. Prior to the home visit at which the observation is conducted, parents are provided information about the purpose of the observation and are informed about the types of activities that will be observed.

At the time of the home visit, rapport is established with the parent and information that was shared initially is reviewed and discussed further. While video recording is not required, it can provide a useful tool for intervention. Materials provided by the assessor to conduct the observation include three board books for the Book Activity and a 5-x-7 blanket. A non-activated recorder that

plays pre-recorded musical tunes every seven seconds is provided for the Distraction Task. The recorder is attached to a brightly colored key chain with keys. The Dressing activity and the Free-Play activity do not require any assessment materials, as the purpose of these activities is to observe typical routines for the parent and child.

Scoring

Each item is scored on a scale of 0 to 3, where 0 = never, 1 = rarely, 2 = sometimes or inconsistently, and 3 = often and consistently. For example, if a parent does not make any descriptive comments during the observation, a score of '0' would be assigned for Descriptive Language. Then, a score is generated for each domain (i.e., Parent Facilitators, Parent Interrupters, Child Engagement, and Child Distress) by summing the scores across the Key Elements for a particular domain and dividing the summed score by the total possible for that domain. This yields a domain percentage score for each observation. These results recorded over time can then be entered into Excel to produces a graph displaying a performance record of growth or change for both parent and child domain scores (Figures 1 and 2) as well as Key Elements that comprise each domain.

Application

IPCI results can be used by early intervention practitioners such as Jodi to make data-based decisions regarding intervention. A Decision-Making Model was developed to assist practitioners in using IGDIs such as the IPCI for this purpose (McConnell et al., 1998). This model, based on previous models for use with General Outcomes Measurement (Kaminski & Good, 1996), serves four purposes: (1) to monitor growth/change; (2) to signal the need for implementation of or modification of intervention to promote parent/ caregiver responsiveness; (3) to evaluate growth/change in parent and child behavior once a new intervention has been introduced or once the intervention is intensified or otherwise modified; and (4) to continue monitoring parent and child progress over time (Carta et al., 2002).

The sooner that practitioners can identify risky interactions, the sooner intervention can be provided to support more positive parent-child interaction, thereby contributing to more positive child social-emotional trajectories over time.

Intervention that reflects data-based decision-making can be especially important for very young children and their families. When early parent-child interactions veer off course, they are not likely to self-correct without intervention (Hofacker & Papousek, 1998). When parent-child interactions fall outside typical limits—that is, when children, especially those who have a disability condition or who are at risk, experience interactions with parents that are significantly lower in responsiveness as compared to parent responsiveness of typically developing children—they have fewer opportunities to make social-emotional gains. Furthermore, discrepancies between these two groups of children's social-emotional trajectories tend to widen with the disability or at-risk group falling further and further behind (Landry et al., 2001). Hence, the sooner that practitioners can identify risky interactions, the sooner intervention can be provided to support more positive parent-child interaction, thereby contributing to more positive child social-emotional trajectories over time.

Checking growth in the responsiveness of parents' and other primary caregivers' interactions with their children is vital to understanding if and how parents and children are benefiting from early intervention aimed at promoting child social-emotional competencies through responsive interactions.

To maximize potential for data-based decision-making, Jodi began administering the IPCI once every 3 months with each child on her caseload to monitor parent-child interaction. For some children, Jodi found that all parent-child interaction domain scores were within typical limits. Jodi was encouraged by this and continued to monitor on a quarterly basis so that she could identify risky interactions should they begin to emerge.

For another group of children, Jodi noticed that domain scores for either Parent Facilitators or Parent Interrupters were falling just outside typical limits. In these cases, Jodi decided to increase quarterly monitoring to monthly monitoring so that in conjunction with other assessment data she could get a picture of whether the atypical scores were a consistent pattern or simply reflecting an" off day."

In the course of monitoring, Jodi became particularly concerned about parent-child interaction for one child, Shawna, and her mother. Consistent with other assessment data indicating concerns, IPCI results showed that during the first quarter of entering the Early Head Start Program, Shawna's results were significantly below the expected level for Child Engagement (see Figure 1). In addition,

Figure 1
IPCI Child Domain Graph: Engagement

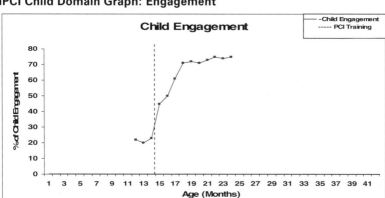

Note: This report shows Shawna's IPCI Engagement scores over time. The first 3 data points reflect IPCI monitoring before intervention while the data points to the right of the dotted line show Shawna's growth in Engagement after beginning intervention.

Parent Facilitators were significantly below the expected level and Interrupters were significantly above the expected level. Next, Jodi looked at the Key Elements of Parent Facilitators and Interrupters so that she could identify relative strengths and concerns for Shawna and her mother. Jodi sought out reflective supervision with an infant mental health specialist at her agency to look at the data with her and to begin developing an intervention plan to support more positive interactions between Shawna and her mother. While the IPCI does not require video recording for scoring purposes, Jodi did video record IPCI assessments so that she could then use them as an intervention tool. Jodi began by sharing the video with Shawna's mother to point out strengths that were identified by the Key Elements graphs. This gave Jodi an opportunity to not only point out a relative strength (e.g., Conveging Acceptance/Warmth) but how it served to help her daughter to engage during the video and how that form of engagement is related to an important family value, Shawna's readiness for school. Jodi and Shawna's mother worked out a plan whereby Shawna's mother would continue to practice the newly identified behavior between home visits. Jodi continued to conduct monthly IPCI assessments and to video record them so that she and Shawna's mother could look at them together along with data reports to see target behaviors grow over time. As Shawna's mother's confidence began to grow, Jodi began to target Key Elements significantly below the expected level (e.g., following child's lead and using descriptive language). Jodi and Shawna's mother continued to look together at Domain graphs and video examples of parent and child behavior during visits. In this way, Jodi was able to use IPCI reports (Figure 2) to

Figure 2
IPCI Parent Domain Graph

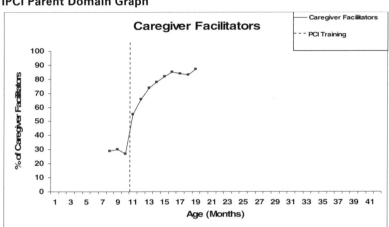

Note: This report shows Jodi how Shawna's mother's positive behaviors are growing with
intervention. It also allows Jodi to show Shawna's mother how, as her behavior changes, her
daughter's positive engagement grows, as illustrated in Figure 1.

*encourage Shawna's mother to try out specific new skills, celebrate
with Shawna's mother as parent responsiveness and child engagement grew, or consult further with the mental health specialist to
modify the intervention for Shawna and her mother.*

Programs need to know when parents and other primary caregivers
are making progress in interactions that foster social-emotional growth
of their very young children. This is essential for programs to recognize
and support parents and primary caregivers in their responsive roles with
their children. Programs also need to know when to provide additional
supports to help parents and primary caregivers respond in ways that
foster positive social-emotional behaviors in their children. Checking
growth in the responsiveness of parents' and other primary caregivers'
interactions with their children is vital to understanding if and how parents and children are benefiting from early intervention aimed at promoting child social-emotional competencies through responsive interactions.
This article describes the IPCI as an example of an IGDI that can be used
to guide intervention decision-making by first monitoring to determine
when and if intervention is warranted, to evaluate effects of intervention
once it is initiated or modified in some way, and to continue monitoring.
Information about the reliability, validity, and sensitivity of this IGDI as
well as other IGDIs for young children can be found online at http://www.
igdi.ku.edu/

Notes

Preparation of this manuscript was supported by The Centers for Evidence-based Practice: Young Children with Challenging Behavior funded by the U.S. Department of Education, Office of Special Education. The authors would like to thank all the IPCI team members who contributed to conceptualization and field testing including Dr. Eva Horn, Dr. Kere Hughes, Gwiok Kim, Rashida Banerjee, Yumiko Saito, and Jeanie Schiefelbusch. In addition, our partnership with Project EAGLE staff and advocates has been invaluable in providing feedback about the IPCI.

Kathleen M. Baggett can be reached by e-mail at kbaggett@ku.edu

References

Appleyard, K., Egeland, B., van Dulmen, M. H., & Sroufe, L. A. (2005). When more is not better: The role of cumulative risk in child behavior outcomes. *Journal of Child Psychology and Psychiatry*, 46(3), 235-245.

Bricker, D., Schoen Davis, M. S., & Squires, J. (2004). Mental health screening in young children. *Infants and Young Children*, 17, 129-144.

Briggs-Gowan, M. J., Carter, A. S., Irwin, J. R., Wachtel, K., & Cicchetti, D.V. (2004). The Brief Infant-Toddler Social and Emotional Assessment: Screening for Social-Emotional Problems and Delays in Competence. *Journal of Pediatric Psychology*, 29, 143-155.

Brooks-Gunn, J., Berlin, L., Fuligni, A., & Sidle, A. (2000). Early childhood intervention programs: What about the family? In J. P. Shonkoff & S. J. Meisels (Eds), *Handbook of early childhood intervention* (2nd ed., pp. 549-588). New York: Cambridge University Press.

Carta, J. J., Greenwood, C. R., Luze, G. J., Cline, G., & Kuntz, S. (2004). Developing a general outcome measure of growth in social skills for infants and toddlers. *Journal of Early Intervention*, 26, 91-114.

Carta, J. J., Greenwood, C. R., Walker, D., Kaminski, R., Good, R., McConnell, S., & McEvoy, M. (2002). Individual Growth and Development Indicators (IGDIs): Assessment that guides intervention for young children. *Young Exceptional Children Monograph Series 4*, 15-28.

Chang, L., Schwartz, D., Dodge, K. A., & McBride-Chang, C. (2003). Harsh parenting in relation to child emotion regulation and aggression. *Journal of Family Psychology*, 17, 598-606.

Deno, S., (1997). Whether thou goest...Perspectives on progress monitoring. In J.W. Lloyd, E.J. Kameenui, & D. Chard (Eds.), *Issues in educating students with disabilities* (pp. 77-99). Mahwah, NJ: Erlbaum.

Greenwood, C. R., Carta, J. J., & Walker, D. (2005). Individual growth and development indicators: Tools for assessing intervention results for infants and toddlers. In W.L. Heward et al. (Eds.), *Focus on Behavior Analysis in Education: Achievements, Challenges, and Opportunities*. Columbus, OH: Merrill.

Hofacker, N. & Papousek, M. (1998). Disorders of excessive crying, feeding, and sleeping: The Munich Interdisciplinary Research and Intervention Program. *Infant Mental Health Journal*, 19(2), 180-201.

Kaminski, R. A. & Good, R. H. (1996). Toward a Technology for Assessing Basic Early Literacy Skills. *School Psychology Review*, 25, 215-227.

Landry, S. H., Smith, K. E., & Swank, P. R. (in press).Responsive parenting: Establishing foundations for social, communication and independent problem-solving. *Developmental Psychology*.

Landry, S. H., Smith, K. E., Swank, P. R., Assel, M. A., & Vellet, N. S. (2001). Does early responsive parenting have a special importance for children's development or is consistency across early childhood necessary? *Developmental Psychology*, 37(3), 387-403.

McConnell, S., McEvoy, M., Carta, J., Greenwood, C., Kaminski, R., Good, R., & Shinn, M. (1998). Theoretical foundations for the Early Childhood Research Institute on measuring growth and development: An early childhood problem-solving model. (Technical Report #6). Minneapolis, MN: University of Minnesota. (ERIC Document Reproduction Service No. 452640).

McConnell, S. R., Priest, J. S., Davis, S. D., & McEvoy, M. A. (2001). Best practices in measuring growth and development for preschool children. In A. Thomas & J. Grimes (Eds.), *Best Practices in School Psychology IV* (Vol. 2, pp. 1231-1246). Bethesda, MD: National Association of School Psychologists.

Meisels, S. J. & Atkins-Burnett, S. (2001). The elements of early childhood assessment. In J.P. Shonkoff & S. J. Meisels (Eds.), *Handbook of Early Intervention* (2nd ed.. pp. 231-257). Cambridge, UK: Cambridge University Press.

Raver, C.C. (2003). *Young Children's Emotional Development and School Readiness*. Champaign, IL: ERIC Clearinghouse on Elementary and Early Childhood Education.

van den Boom, D. C. (1994). The influence of temperament and mothering on attachment and exploration: An experimental manipulation of sensitive responsiveness among lower-class mothers with irritable infants. *Child Development*, 65(5), 1457-1477.

van den Boom D. C. (1995). Do first-year intervention effects endure? Follow-up during toddlerhood of a sample of Dutch irritable infants. *Child Development*, 66, 1798-1816.

Pets in the Classroom

Promoting and Enhancing Social-Emotional Wellness of Young Children

Brinda Jegatheesan, Ph.D.,
University of Washington

Hedda Meadan, Ph.D.,
Illinois State University

During Tuesday morning group time, Mrs. Ramu introduced two new classmates to the children, a pair of brown and black furry hamsters. The pair of hamsters joined the rest of the animal family in the classroom, which included Momo the turtle and Nico, Yolanda, and Shir, the three goldfish. Mrs. Ramu looked at the 17 excited young children sitting on the carpet. "So what should we call them?" asked Mrs. Ramu. She put a picture of each hamster on the board and wrote the names that the children suggested next to each picture. By the end of group time two names were chosen, Browny and Blacky.

Over the next few days, the preschoolers learned about what hamsters eat, where they like to eat, and how they like to be petted. Mrs. Ramu read books about hamsters and created different center time activities related to hamsters (e.g., a matching game with hamster pictures, puppets of hamsters in the animal hospital dramatic play center). In addition, Momo the turtle, the pair of hamsters, and the fish tank were available as choice time for the children. Kenny, a 4-year-old boy with autism who loved Momo the turtle, pointed to the picture of Momo when it was his turn to select his center activity. Mrs. Ramu smiled and sent Kenny to Momo's box. A few minutes later Latisa, a 3-year-old girl, joined Kenny at Momo's box. Kenny and Latisa, with the help of Joy, the paraprofessional in the class, picked up the turtle and gently petted him. Joy showed Kenny three pictures—lettuce, ice, and rocks. She then asked him to point to the food that Momo liked. Kenny looked at the pictures and touched the picture of the lettuce. Latisa reached for the bowl of lettuce and together the two children fed Momo. In another corner of the classroom, Varon and Billy sat next to the fish tank and were busy painting watercolor pictures of the three fish swimming in and out of the green weeds. They were *talking softly with each other trying to identify each of the three fish by their names.*

The above example illustrates how classroom pets assisted Mrs. Ramu to facilitate the inclusion and participation of all the children in the classroom. She was able to assist Kenny, a child with limited expressive language, to communicate his wants and ideas. She also helped Varon, who had difficulties staying on task, remain calm and focused as he spent time doing his favorite activity, painting. Both children also had the opportunity to interact and communicate with other children in the classroom.

This article introduces the idea of companion animals in the classroom to support inclusion and social-emotional development of young children with special needs and at risk. We begin with a definition of Animal-Assisted Therapy (AAT). We describe the early origins of AAT and the potential benefits of classroom pets on young children's development. Pet-assisted classroom activities and information for enhancing the early childhood curriculum and routines are provided. Interacting with pets should be viewed as complementary to human interaction and building relationships (Melson, 2001). It should not be viewed as a replacement for adult-child or child-adult interactions. A discussion of necessary precautions, both for the welfare of children and the animals in the classroom is also included.

> ■──────────────■
> *Animal-Assisted Activities (AAA) provide opportunities for the overall enhancement of an individual's quality of life. These include educational and motivational benefits.*

Animal-Assisted Therapy

Animal-Assisted Therapy (AAT) is a goal-directed intervention. Health and human service professionals utilize animals that meet certain criteria to assist in the intervention process. A premise of many AAT programs is that animals have an invaluable role in promoting social and behavioral changes in young children. Such changes include the acquisition of nurturing and social skills, a sense of responsibility, the ability to regulate impulsive/disruptive behavior, and a feeling of positive self-esteem (Kruger, Trachtenberg, & Serpell, 2004).

Animal-Assisted Activities (AAA) provide opportunities for the overall enhancement of an individual's quality of life. These include educational and motivational benefits. Activities are planned and delivered in a range

Table 1
Organizations That Support Animals in Classrooms

American Society for the Prevention of Cruelty to Animals (www.aspca.org/site)
Delta Society (www. Deltasociety.org)
Green Chimneys (greenchimneys.org)
The Humane Society of the United States (www.hsus.org)
The Latham Foundation for the Promotion of Humane Education (www.latham. org)

of environments by trained persons, who have knowledge of animals and prior association with them (Kruger et al., 2004).

Background and History of Animal-Assisted Therapy

Animals have always been used by human beings, usually for food and then for transportation. When people began to live in villages, more than 15,000 years ago, an additional role included companionship (Beck, 2000). Levinson (1980) argued that

> ...by domesticating an animal man demonstrated his kinship with nature. ... Psychologically this was the beginning of a symbolic relationship between pets and human beings in which man supplied the material needs of the pet while the pet satisfied the psychological needs of his master (p. 63).

Most people date the beginning of the modern interest in human-animal interactions to Boris Levinson's first research paper on this topic, entitled "The dog as a co-therapist" (1962). Levinson, a child psychologist, accidentally discovered the benefits of animals in therapy while treating a child who was severely withdrawn. One day the child and his mother came for their therapy session earlier than expected. Levinson's dog, who was with him at that time, was instrumental in breaking the child's silence. This event was the beginning of a new era of psychoanalytical inquiry wherein Levinson took the lead in the professional development of psychotherapeutic practice, establishing the term 'human-companion animal therapy.' The formal introduction and documentation of the potential benefits of using animals as a communication link between therapists and children was established.

Table 2
Suggested Activities by Social-Emotional Developmental Area

Social-Emotional Development Area	Activities
Compassion and responsibility	• Take turns cleaning the cage or feeding the pet. Keep a record on the classroom Pet Wellness Chart. • Observe the animal in different situations (e.g., investigate preferred foods and sleeping areas). Discuss and chart observations. • Talk about/chart how our behavior and actions affect the animal's responses such as trust, loyalty, acceptance, friendship.
Social interaction	• Create pet puzzle from art work. • Create an animal learning center where children come together and share stories about their favorite pet or special stories about a pet. • Vote for the "special pet of the month" and then work together to make a collage, art and paint work combined with creative writing and hang in the school corridor.
Self-esteem and self-worth	• Create a "classroom tree" chart, with a leaf bearing each child's name. Children can have their achievements for the week (e.g., cleaning the cage, feeding pets) written on their individual leaf.
Awareness of one's own and others' feelings	• Talk about how pets feel, under what circumstances, and how they behave (e.g., why do turtles slip inside their shell). • Role-play to understand pets and their emotion. • Read books on animals and feelings.

Potential Contributions for Children with Special Needs

Jacobsen (as cited in Cusack, 1988) identified seven functions that animals can fulfill in the educational and therapeutic areas for *children with disabilities*. The animals provide (1) emotional support, (2) behavior control, (3) socialization skills, (4) assistance with physical competency, (5) assistance with mobility problems, (6) responsibility training, and (7) motivation and content for education in academic skills. In addition, through interactions between children and pets, animals can assist teachers to (1) develop a deeper understanding of students, (2) enhance bonding, and (3) at times uncover hidden problems in students.

Social-Emotional Development

This article focuses on the social-emotional development of young children at risk and with disabilities with the assistance of classroom pets. Quality early education environments are related to positive outcomes in young children's social and emotional development. Such environments allow children to explore, learn, and grow developmentally (Sandall, Hemmeter, Smith, & McLean, 2005; Bredekamp & Copple, 1997). Adding animals to the classroom environment can support other effective practices that enhance social-emotional development. Melson (2001) reported that children ranked pets as their most intimate affective connection and stated that their pets were one of the 10 most important figures in their lives. The practice of having classroom pets, while not uncommon, is beginning to gain attention in its impact on children's overall development. A partial list of organizations that support animals in classrooms is presented in Table 1.

Adding animals to the classroom environment can support other effective practices that enhance social-emotional development.

This article addresses four important areas of social-emotional development: (1) developing compassion and responsibility, (2) promoting and facilitating social interactions, (3) developing and enhancing self-esteem and self-worth, and (4) promoting awareness of one's own and others' feelings. With both typically developing children and children with special needs, research has shown that social-emotional development can be enhanced through interaction with pets (Jalongo, Robbins, & Stanek, 2004; Kruger et al., 2004).

Develop Compassion and Responsibility

Having pets in the classroom provides opportunities for children to understand how the wellness of their pets depends on the child's ability to provide care and attention. Development of awareness and empathy helps children to be caring and nurturing individuals (Melson, 2001; Rud & Beck, 2000). Teachers can use this caregiving to encourage children to learn about and develop skills in caring and become cognizant of different needs and abilities. In the opening vignette, Mrs. Ramu was able to achieve this by teaching the food habits, living environment, and petting styles specific to hamsters. Responsibilities such as cleaning cages, filling water bowls, feeding, and spending time with pets help children take the role of caregivers.

Through caregiving practice, children can begin to understand the different needs of their pets and learn the importance of giving care and love (Melson, 2001). Melson has suggested that the development of sensitivity and a nurturing personality is an important underpinning for caring and assisting others who are in need (e.g., children with special needs). Other studies report greater empathy towards peers when children were taught to be nurturing (Ascione, 1992; Melson, Peet, & Sparks, 1992). Furthermore, children view the task of caring for their pets as gender-neutral, which allows boys and girls to be equally receptive and gives boys an opportunity to be nurturing and caring (Checchi, 1999; Melson, 2001).

Teachers can plan supervised activities that enhance responsibility and caring. The teacher and children can talk as a class about what needs to be cleaned, replenished, and fixed so that the pets will be comfortable in the class. In addition, they can discuss the general well-being of the pets and what children can do to make the animals happier. Table 2 presents additional examples of classroom activities, as well as examples of activities related to social interactions, developing self-esteem, and awareness of feelings – areas discussed later in this paper.

Teachers play a crucial role in modeling appropriate behaviors and interactions with classroom pets. Teachers can help children understand the importance of the care they provide by communicating with children about their responsibilities (e.g., why it is important to remember to clean the cage), feelings (e.g., how Blacky the hamster will feel if there is no drinking water), and empathy (e.g., why Momo the turtle put his head inside his shell).

Table 3
List of Recommended Readings

- Fine, A (2000). *Handbook of animal-assisted therapy*. San Diego, CA: Academic Press.
- Gunnels, J.A. (1997). A class pet campaign: Experiencing the democratic process. *Dimensions of Early Childhood, 25*, 31-34.
- Hodges, J.L. (1991). Spiders and boas and rats, oh my! *Science and Children, 28* (4), 22-25.
- Hurst, C.O. (1998). Dogs, cats, and other fauna. *Teaching Pre-k–8, 18*(5), 74.
- Kramer, D.C. (1989). *Animals in the classroom: Selection, care and observations*. Reading, MA: Addison-Wesley.
- Melson, G. (2001). *Why the wild things are: Animals in the lives of children*. Cambridge, MA: Harvard University Press.

Table 4

Teacher Checklist for Classroom Pets (Adapted from Classroom Pets Checklist, Ontario SPCA Humane Education, http:// www.ospca.on.ca/ he_ft.html#classroompets)

- Are you willing to be the primary caretaker of the pet?
- Do you have adequate knowledge of pets or have had prior experience with them?
- Are you comfortable in caring for and handling pets?
- Do you know the objectives of having a classroom pet?
- Have you considered school policies and written liability on having pets in your classroom?
- Will the pet do well in a classroom with different kinds of children?
- Do you have students with severe allergies?
- Is there enough space to have a home for the pet in the classroom?
- Have you considered who will be financially responsibility of providing care?
- Are you willing to take the pet into your home during weekends and vacations?
- Are you willing to give time, energy, and money to provide care when the pet is sick?
- Most important, are you committed to the lifetime of the pet?

Promote and Facilitate Social Interactions

Children acquire a range of skills through hands-on interactive activities. The use of listening, imitating, and questioning skills expands their ability to take part in meaningful interactions and engage in a range of social experiences (Blaustein, 2005). When children work in pairs or as a group toward something that motivates, excites, and captivates them, they forget about individual differences and work towards a common goal. Activities that focus on pets facilitate interactions, acceptance, companionship, and mutual enjoyment. Children feel the joy of shared learning (Rud & Beck, 2000; Twiest, Twiest, & Jalongo, 2004). Working together builds a sense of community, which in turn fosters feelings of belonging, membership, and commitment toward supporting one another. Teachers can encourage social interaction by pairing children when taking care of the animals or facilitating group discussions related to the animals. We see how Mrs. Ramu carefully crafted an opportunity for Kenny and Latisa to interact with one another in meaningful ways and to experience learning in an inclusive environment. Classroom pets assisted Mrs. Ramu in her goal of creating an environment that supported relationships and a feeling of community.

Develop and Enhance Self-Esteem and Self-Worth

Nurturing and supporting children's sense of self is important in early childhood development. Katz (1995, as cited in Bredekamp & Copple,

1997) talks about having a unit in the classroom called, "I am special." Having an environment that supports the feeling of being special is important. Such a sense can be attained through the accomplishment of simple tasks, which can bring great pride and joy and can also promote a sense of confidence, competence and self-worth. For example, teachers can encourage children to talk during 'show and tell' time about something special they did for their classroom pets. Teachers can persuade children to share their observations of how the pet responded to them and express their feelings at their pet's reaction to what they did. We also see how Mrs. Ramu bolstered the confidence of the children by first providing them with information about hamsters and then designing dramatic play centers for them to participate in. During this time children can be persuaded to role-play the vet, pet food consultant, vet nurse, and other pet-related roles.

When children are emotionally invested in an activity, they go to great lengths to complete it. Melson (2001) states that a "primary function of human social support is to communicate a sense that others love, value, and care about you...pets...fulfill that role for many children" (p. 61). Some highly interactive pets (e.g., dogs, hamsters) play a pivotal role in enhancing a child's self-worth. They make children feel needed, missed, and important. According to Rud and Beck (2000), there is evidence that animals can change a child's "attitude towards him or herself and improve the ability to relate to others" (p. 313).

Promote Awareness of One's Own and Others' Feelings

The bond between children and pets helps children become better able to express their feelings and emotions. Melson (2001) stated that children turn to their pets for comfort and reassurance when they are sad, afraid, or upset. Melson highlights that children's conversations with pets typically involve touch. In clinical settings, therapists have continually emphasized the comfort that children find in petting and stroking furry, soft pets. Children also believe that animals understand them and this makes it easy for youngsters to talk about their anxiety, shyness, and fear and become better able to express their thoughts. Pets then become the "uncritical, accepting audience that invites disclosure" (Melson, 2001, p. 48). Robin and Bensel (1985) stated that since children demonstrate a

Since children demonstrate a greater need for empathetic listening, the non-intervention nature and empathy of pets makes them ideal companions to provide emotional support.

Table 5
Tips for Classroom Pet Selection (Adapted from Twiest, Twiest, & Jalongo, 2004)

Pets	Diet	Personality	Care	Life Span
Hamster	Hamster food, fresh fruit and vegetables, hay	Interactive when awake, sociable, likes being held and petted	Easy to care, clean, inexpensive to feed, requires exercise	2–3 years
Turtle	Some plants/ small fish, fish eggs, turtle food	Sociable, quiet, interactive	Easy to care, clean, inexpensive to feed	70–100 years
Guinea pig	Fresh fruit and vegetables, corn & pellets	Sociable, interactive, inquisitive, calm, and observant	Regular exercise, clean and quiet habitat	5–7 years
Fish	Fish food	Calm, observable	Regular change in water	2–3 years
Lizard	Fresh fruit and vegetables, commercially available small insects, calcium supplements	Good to observe, does not like handling	Heating and infra-lighting needed	Varies

greater need for empathetic listening, the non-intervention nature and empathy of pets makes them ideal companions to provide emotional support. Children's interaction with their pets and the reciprocity of the pets to their behaviors and actions builds a greater awareness of their own internal states.

Pets in the classroom can help remove gender-based stereotypical attitudes about appropriate emotional expressions and patterns of interactions. Bonds with animals allow boys to express feelings as they care for pets. Animals also provide an avenue for emotional support and feelings of security (Bryant, 1985; Checchi, 1999). Creany (2004) states that caring for animals can provide comfort to a boy by soothing his "concerns and worries without exposing his fears" (p. 37).

Some children turn towards their pets for private time to find comfort and solace. Levinson's pioneering work demonstrated the role a pet can play with young children with special needs (Levinson, 1962). Since then, other researchers have documented that children find emotional comfort in their relationships with animals and how, with little inhibition, they talk to their hamsters, gerbils, and birds about their fears, joys, angers, dreams, and the everyday issues important to them (Bryant, 1985; Covert, Whirren, Keith, & Nelson, 1985; Mallon, 1992; Melson & Schwarz, 1994). It has been noted that children's contact with animals is almost universally beneficial (Beck & Katcher, 1983). Parents have reported that their children who found such support from their pets were less anxious (Melson, 2001). Children appeared to "use their pets as calming time-outs and restorers of equilibrium" (p. 60).

Health Benefits of Animals

Researchers also have investigated the health benefits of animals. Friedmann (2000) reviewed the literature and concluded that "evidence supports the proposition that animals enhance health" (p. 53). Different types of interactions with animals have specific health effects. Owning a pet was associated with cardiovascular health. Looking at or observing an animal was associated with a decrease in physiologic arousal and increased feelings of happiness. The presence of an animal was found to be associated with a decrease in anxiety and depression (Friedmann, 2000). These health benefits may assist students who exhibit either externalizing (increased attention- seeking behaviors) or internalizing (decreased physiologic arousal and depression) problem behavior.

Making Decisions about Having Pets as Part of Classroom Environment

It is important for teachers to consider the issues related to the ideology and the practice of having pets in the classroom. In addition to exploring the websites of the organizations presented in Table 1, teachers may refer to the readings listed in Table 3. Addressing the questions presented in Table 4 can assist a teacher in deciding if adding pets to the classroom environment is appropriate for and desired by all the stakeholders. Deciding which animal to include in the classroom environment (e.g., Kramer, 1989) is another important step. Tips for classroom pet selection are presented in Table 5. Finally, teachers need to carefully plan for the inclusion of the pets in the classroom. Although this article focuses on the role of pets in the promotion and enhancement of the social-emotional development of young children, teachers might consider including pets in activities that promote other areas, such as literacy, art, and science (e.g., Hodges 1991; Hurst, 1998; Lewin-Benham, 2006).

Alternative Ways of Having Classroom Animal Companions

School rules, children's allergies, or teacher preferences may not allow pets in the classroom. In such cases, teachers can have an open discussion with children and choose an alternate way of having a pet. One example would be to adopt a real wild animal for a chosen period of time through the World Wildlife Fund (WWF). The organization sends a picture of the chosen animal, species fact sheets, WWF screensavers, greetings cards and quarterly updates on how the animal is faring (http://www.wwf.org.uk/adoption/index.asp).

Conclusions

With the passage of the No Child Left Behind (NCLB) Act of 2001, there has been a strong emphasis on developing the cognitive skills of young children to increase their academic achievements (Cook, Klein, & Tessier, 2004). Given this current emphasis on academic content and skills, it is important not to overlook young children's social-emotional development, which is an important prerequisite of school readiness, adjustment, and academic success (Webster-Stratton & Reid, 2004). Classroom pets can provide children with real experiences to promote, nurture, and affirm a healthy sense of self. To this end, we propose the presence of pets in the classroom to enhance the social-emotional development of young children.

Note

You can reach Brinda Jegatheesan by email at brinda@u.washington.edu

References

Ascione, F. (1992). Enhancing children's attitudes about the humane treatment of animals: Generalization to human-directed empathy. *Anthrozoos, 5,* 176-191.

Beck, A., & Katcher, A. H. (1983). *Between pets and people: The importance of animal companionship.* New York: Putnam.

Beck, A. M. (2000). The use of animals to benefits humans: Animal-assisted therapy. In A. Fine (Ed.), *Handbook on animal-assisted therapy: Theoretical foundations and guidelines for practice* (pp. 21-40). San Diego, CA: Academic Press.

Blaustein, M. (2005, July). See, hear, touch! The basics of learning readiness. *Beyond the Journal—Young Children on the Web.* 1-10. Retrieved on June 30, 2006, from http://www.maineaeyc.org/uploads/The%20Basics%20of%20Learning%20Readiness.pdf

Bredekamp, S. & Copple, C. (1997). *Developmentally appropriate practice in early childhood programs.* Washington, DC: National Association for the Education of Young Children (NAEYC).

Bryant, B. (1985). The neighborhood walk: Sources of support in middle childhood. *Monographs of the Society for Research in Child Development, 50,* No. 210.

Checchi, M. J. (1999). *Are the pets for me?* New York: St. Martin's Press.

Cook, R., Klein, D., & Tessier, A. (2004). Adapting early childhood curricula for children in inclusive settings. Columbus, OH: Pearson Prentice Hall.

Covert, A. M., Whirren, A. P., Keith, J., & Nelson, C. (1985). Pets, early adolescents, and families. *Marriage and Family Review, 8,* 95-108.

Creany, A. D. (2004). Companion animals in the lives of boys and girls: Gendered attitudes, practices, and preferences. In M. Jalongo (Ed.), *The world's children and their companion animals: Developmental and education significance of the child/pet bond* (pp. 35-46). Olney, MD: Association for Childhood Education International.

Cusack, D. (1988). *Pets and mental health*. Haworth Press: N.Y.

Friedmann, E. (2000). The animal-human bond: Health and wellness. In A. Fine (Ed.), *Handbook on animal-assisted therapy: Theoretical foundations and guidelines for practice* (pp. 41-58). San Diego, CA: Academic Press.

Hodges, J. L. (1991). Spiders and boas and rats, oh my! *Science and Children*, 28(4), 22-25.

Hurst, C. O. (1998). Dogs, cats, and other fauna. *Teaching Pre-k–8, 18* (5), 74.

Jalongo, M., Robbins, R., & Paterno, R. (2004). The special significance of companion animals in children's lives. In M. Jalongo (Ed.), *The world's children and their companion animals: Developmental and education significance of the child/pet bond* (pp. 9-19). Olney, MD: Association for Childhood Education International.

Kramer, D. C. (1989). *Animals in the classroom: Selection, care and observations*. Reading, MA: Addison-Wesley.

Kruger, K. A., Trachtenberg, S. W., Serpell, J. A. (2004). *Can animals help humans heal? Animal-assisted interventions in adolescent mental health*. Center for Interaction of Animals and Society, University of Pennsylvania School of Veterinary Medicine. Retrieved March 3, 2006, from http://www2.vet.upenn.edu/research/centers/cias /store.htm

Levinson, B. M. (1962). The dog as co-therapist. *Mental Hygiene, 46*, 59-65.

Levinson, B. M. (1980). The child and his pet: A world of nonverbal communication. In S.A. Corson & O.E. Corson (Eds.), *Etiology and Nonverbal Communication in Mental Health* (pp. 63-81). Pergamon Press.

Lewin-Benham, A. (2006). One teacher, 20 preschoolers, and a goldfish. *Young Children, 61*(2), 28-34.

Mallon, G. (1992). Utilization of animals as therapeutic adjuncts with children and youth: A review of the literature. *Child and Youth Care Forum, 21*(1), 53-67.

Melson, G. F. (2001). *Why the wild things are: Animals in the lives of children*. Cambridge, MA: Harvard University Press.

Melson, G. F., Peet, S., & Sparks, C. (1992). Children's attachment to their pets: Links to socioemotional development. *Children's Environments Quarterly, 8*, 55-65.

Melson, G. F., & Schwarz, R. (1994, October). *Pets as social supports for families of young children*. Paper presented at the annual meeting of the Delta Society, New York.

Ontario SPCA (2005). *Ontario SPCA humane education classroom pets: A checklist for teachers*. Retrieved March 3, 2006, from http://www.ospca.on.ca/he_ft.html#classroompets

Robin, M. & Bensel, R. (1985). Pets and the socialization of children. In Sussman, M. (Ed.), *Pets and the family* (pp. 63-77). New York: Haworth Press.

Rud, A. G., & Beck, A. M. (2000). Kids and critters in class together. *Phi Delta Kappan, 82*(4), 313-315.

Sandall, S., Hemmeter, M. L., Smith, B., & McLean, M. (2005). DEC recommended practices: *A comprehensive guide for practical application in early intervention/early childhood special education*. Longmont, CO: Sopris West.

Twiest, M. G., Twiest, M. M., & Jalongo, M. R. (2004). A friend at school: Classroom pets and companion animals in the curriculum. In M. Jalongo (Ed.), *The world's children and their companion animals: Developmental and education significance of the child/pet bond* (pp. 61-78). Olney, MD: Association for Childhood Education International.

Webster-Stratton, C. & Reid, M. J. (2004). Strengthening social and emotional competence in young children—The foundation for early school readiness and success: Incredible years classroom social skills and problem-solving curriculum. *Infants and Young Children, 17* (2), 96-113.

Resources
Within Reason

*Supporting the Social
Competence of Young Children*

Camille Catlett, M.A.,
University of North Carolina at Chapel Hill

Here you'll find additional resources to support the social competence of young children and to assist in developing supports within everyday routines, activities and places. Resources range in price. Many are within an individual's budget while others may be more suitable for acquisition by an agency or program.

Print Resources

Achieving Learning Goals Through Play: Teaching Young Children With Special Needs, (2nd ed.).

A. H. Widerstrom

Play is more than just fun; it's a powerful teaching tool that helps young children learn. With this practical, activity-filled guide, you'll have ready-to-use strategies for weaving individual learning goals into play throughout the school day. Created for use with children ages 2 to 5 who have special needs (but equally effective for typically developing children), *Achieving Learning Goals Through Play* provides information on how play activities can help children develop cognitive, communication, motor, social, and pre-literacy skills.

> Brookes Publishing
> P.O. Box 10624
> Baltimore, MD 21285-0624
> (800) 638-3775
> FAX: (410) 337-8539
> Web site: http://www.brookespublishing.com

Designing Early Intervention Programs to Promote Children's Social Competence
M. J. Guralnick & B. Neville (in M. J. Guralnick [Ed.], The effectiveness of early intervention)

In this chapter from Guralnick's highly significant text, *The Effectiveness of Early Intervention* (1997), Guralnick and Neville assert that social competence is a valued outcome of early intervention programs; it provides a "systematic basis for organizing and structuring" curricular activities, the development of support systems for families, and the incorporation of cultural experiences in children's learning.

Brookes Publishing
P.O. Box 10624
Baltimore, MD 21285-0624
(800) 638-3775
FAX: (410) 337-8539
Web site: http://www.brookespublishing.com

Embedding Choices Into the Daily Routines of Young Children With Behavior Problems: Eight Reasons to Build Social Competence
K. Jolivette, K. McCormick, L. A. Jung, & A. S. Lingo

In this 2004 article from the journal *Beyond Behavior*, the authors discuss why it is important to provide daily routine choices for children with behavior problems (though many of the reasons apply to all young children). Reasons emphasized include: promoting independence; teaching children to self-monitor appropriate behaviors; providing a sense of control; improving performance; fostering a positive, general sense of well-being; and linking behavior and values to responsibility.

Fostering Children's Social Competence: The Teacher's Role
L. G. Katz & D. E. McClellan

On an essential topic, this book is both authoritative and accessible to early childhood professionals. Drawing from research and expert practice, Katz and McClellan explain developmental factors in social competence, positive and negative influences on disposition (including negative classroom influences that may surprise you), and suggest principles and strategies for teachers to understand and use to foster social competence.

National Association for the Education of Young Children
1313 L St. N.W. Suite 500, Washington, DC 20005
800-424-2460
Web site: http://sales.naeyc.org/default.aspx

Friendship Development Among Children In School (Language and Learning for Human Service Processions)
Thomas Rizzo

Based on an ethnography of first-graders' friendships, the book addresses two major questions: (1) How does the social-ecology of a public school classroom affect children's interactions and peer relations, and (2) what are the important psychosocial processes by which children initiate and cultivate friendships at school? Published in 1988, Rizzo's book offers hypotheses about the development of friendship among young children and the chain of events through which children come to consider themselves friends. Norwood, NJ: Ablex.

Guiding Children's Social Development: Theory to Practice (4th ed.)
M. J. Kostelnik, A. Whiren, A. Soderman, L. Stein, & K. Gregory

With emphasis on ways professionals can enhance children's social competence and help children develop positive feelings of self-esteem while learning to get along with others, this book offers practical, developmentally appropriate strategies. Published in 2002, it provides extensive explanations of how to translate these strategies into practical classroom skills and suggests procedures that can be used to increase student or practitioner effectiveness in the classroom.

Delmar Publishers
Thomson Learning
Attn: Order Fulfillment
P.O. Box 6904
Florence, KY 41022
(800) 347-7707
FAX: (800) 487-8488
Web site: http://www.earlychilded.delmar.com

How to Promote Children's Social and Emotional Competence
C. Webster-Stratton

This book, published in 1999, is for teachers of children between 4 and 8 years of age. It shows how teachers can collaborate with parents in addressing children's educational and emotional needs. The author, who believes that children's emotional literacy is as important as academic literacy, presents various classroom management strategies that teachers can select to strengthen children's social and academic competence.

Sage Publications
2455 Teller Road
Thousand Oaks, CA 91320
800-818-7243
FAX: 800-583-2665
Web site: http://www.sagepub.com

Let's Be Friends: Peer Competence and Social Inclusion in Early Childhood Programs
K. M. Kemple

Let's Be Friends (2004) addresses critical questions about how early child-hood programs can help all young children, including those at risk, to develop competent social interaction skill; the book offers "an invaluable contribution in its translation of research results into practical interven-tions." Combining current knowledge of general early childhood educa-tion and early childhood special education, this unique volume explains a wide variety of strategies that range from environmental arrangement, on-the-spot teaching, and cooperative learning, to more intensive, indi-vidually-targeted interventions. "Food for thought" exercises at the end of each chapter can be used as assignments by faculty or as reflections by readers.

Teachers College Press
P.O. Box 20
Williston, VT 05495-0020
(800) 575-6566
(802) 864-7626
Web site: http://store.tcpress.com

The Promoting Alternative Thinking Strategies (PATHS) Curriculum
C. A. Kusche & M. T. Greenberg

PATHS (Promoting Alternative THinking Strategies) is a comprehensive program for promoting emotional and social competencies and reducing aggression and acting-out behaviors in elementary school–aged children while simultaneously enhancing the educational process in the class-room. This innovative curriculum for kindergarten through sixth grade (ages 5 to 12) is used by educators and counselors as a multiyear, preven-tion model. The PATHS curriculum provides teachers with systematic and developmentally based lessons, materials, and instructions for teaching their students emotional literacy, self-control, social competence, positive peer relations, and interpersonal problem-solving skills.

Channing-Bete Company
(800) 477-4776
FAX: (800) 499-6464
Web site: http://www.channing-bete.com/prevention-programs/paths-preschool/

Pathways to Competence
S. Landy

Nine critical aspects of social and emotional development in children from birth to 6 years are covered in this comprehensive reference, published in 2002. Each chapter includes content, principles for caregivers, tips, exercises, activities and additional references (for adults and children). This is a solid resource for building student or caregiver competence.

Brookes Publishing
P.O. Box 10624
Baltimore, MD 21285-0624
(800) 638-3775
FAX: (410) 337-8539
Web site: http://www.brookespublishing.com

Promoting Social Communication in Children And Youth With Developmental Disabilities From Birth to Adolescence
H. Goldstein, L. Kaczmarek, & K. English (Eds.)

Social and communication skills are reciprocal; improving one triggers the development of the other. Published in 2001, this text explores the complex connection between social and communication skills, helping the reader learn to apply the latest research on planning social-communication interventions for children with developmental disabilities. Highlights of the text include research-based strategies with practical case studies and innovative assessment and intervention techniques.

Brookes Publishing
P.O. Box 10624
Baltimore, MD 21285-0624
(800) 638-3775
FAX: (410) 337-8539
Web site: http://www.brookespublishing.com

You Can't Say You Can't Play
V. G. Paley

In this book published in 1992, Vivian Paley employs a unique strategy to probe the moral dimensions of the classroom by extending her analysis to children, kindergarten through the fifth grade, all the while weaving a remarkable fairy tale into her narrative. Answers to questions about fairness and exclusivity ("You can't say you can't play.") are found in the words of creative, insightful children and their wise, attentive teacher. Cambridge, MA: Harvard University Press.

Checklists and Measures

Playmates and Friends Questionnaire
B. D. Goldman & V. Buysse

This questionnaire was designed to document the number and nature of children's relationships with peers in early childhood settings. The questionnaire is divided into three sections: playmates, special friends, and strategies to facilitate friendship formation. The questionnaire, which is being used in the U.S. Department of Education's Cost, Quality and Outcomes of Preschool Inclusion Project, can be completed by a classroom teacher to assist in monitoring an individual child's progress or to develop a specialized intervention. Chapel Hill, NC: FPG Child Development Institute.

> Available online at http://www.fpg.unc.edu/~publicationsoffice/pdfs/playmates_friends_rev.pdf

Young Children's Social Development: A Checklist
Diane McClellan & Lilian G. Katz

Based on research on the relationship of peer relationships, social competence, and cognitive development, the authors designed a Social Attributes checklist to help parents and teachers conduct realistic assessments and support pro-social behaviors that are culturally congruent.

> Available online at http://www.nldontheweb.org/Mcclellan_Katz.htm

Videotapes

To Have a Friend
Portage Project

This video features six minutes of beautiful images of young friends of diverse cultures and abilities in a range of natural environments against a musical backdrop. It could be used to illustrate benefits of inclusion and to explore strategies for encouraging and supporting friendships among all children. Discussion questions, simulation exercises and resource materials are provided in an accompanying booklet.

> CESA-5
> Attn: Portage Project Materials
> P.O. Box 564
> 626 E. Slifer Street
> Portage, Wisconsin 53901
> (800) 862-3725, ext. 221
> FAX: (608) 742-2384
> Web site: http://www.portageproject.org

Promoting First Relationships: A Curriculum for Service Providers to Help Parents and Other Caregivers Meet Young Children's Social and Emotional Needs

J. Kelly, T. Zuckerman, D. Sandoval, & K. Buehlman

What do babies know and need? This 2003 training program (video) and curriculum guide offer specific guidelines for strengthening child-caregiver-provider relationships in ways that meet children's needs, foster development, and enhance feelings of self-worth. A strengths-based approach to caregiving emphasizes the importance of attachments, responsiveness and trust. Attention is given to special needs and abilities. Helpful suggestions are given for developing intervention plans. Collaborative relationships between caregivers and providers are highlighted throughout—in the video, the hand-outs, and the curriculum guide. Reflective questions, observation guides, and hand-outs make these materials a wonderful resource for teachers, parents, and service providers.

NCAST-AVENUW
University of Washington
Box 357920
Seattle, WA 98195-7920
(206) 543-8528
FAX: (206) 685-3284
Web site: http://www.ncast.org/ordering.asp

Promoting Social and Emotional Competence

Center on the Social and Emotional Foundations for Early Learning (CSEFEL)

These modules are based on input from early childhood program administrators, training and technical assistance providers, educators, and family members about the types and content of training that would be most useful in building the social-emotional competence of young children. Download the four modules in English or Spanish at http://csefel.uiuc.edu/modules.html or order them as a set (CD-ROM + videotape).

CSEFEL
61 Children's Research Center
51 Gerty Drive
University of Illinois at Urbana-Champaign
Champaign, IL 61820
(217) 333-4123
FAX: (217) 244-7732
Web site: http://csefel.uiuc.edu

Social-Emotional Growth and Socialization
Center for Child and Family Studies, California Department of Education.

This module is actually a set of integrated materials including a print resource (*Infant/Toddler Caregiving: A Guide to Social-Emotional Growth and Socialization*), three videos (*First Moves, Flexible, Fearful, or Feisty,* and *Getting in Tune*), and a *Trainer's Manual*. Based on current theory and practice, these materials are clearly organized in lesson plans that can be covered in 45 minutes or more. Each lesson plan includes an overview, key concepts in culturally competent child care, materials, activity sheets, handouts, overheads, discussion questions and options for further exploration.

WestEd PITC
80 Harbor Drive, Suite 112
Sausalito, CA 94965-1410
(415) 289-2300
FAX: (415) 289-2301
Web site: http://www.pitc.org/cs/pitclib/print/pitc_docs/products4.html

Web Resources

Assessing Children's Social Competence

Basic, practical information (What is social competence? What makes social competence so important during childhood? How does a child develop social competence?) is provided in English and Spanish at this web site in a question-answer format.

Available online at http://www.illinoisearlylearning.org/faqs/socialcomp.htm (English) or
http://www.illinoisearlylearning.org/faqs-sp/socialcomp-sp.htm (Spanish)

Center for Evidence-Based Practice: Young Children With Challenging Behavior

Handouts, research summaries, training materials and links are some of the resources to be found at this site. Particularly useful are the Recommended Practices Handouts, downloadable and reproducible fact sheets that offer evidence-based recommendations for a variety of topics. Sample topics include Linking Social Development and School Readiness to Behavior and Program Practices for Promoting the Social Development of Young Children.

Available online at http://challengingbehavior.fmhi.usf.edu/resources.html

Center on the Social and Emotional Foundations for Early Learning

If you're looking for a variety of resources, in English and Spanish, to support the social competence of young children, you will thoroughly enjoy this site. The Center has developed evidence-based, user-friendly information, in a variety of forms, to help support childhood educators, parents and administrators. Downloadable resources range from training modules and "what works" briefs to tools and practical strategies.

Available online at http://www.csefel.uiuc.edu

Good beginning: Sending America's Children to School With the Social and Emotional Competence They Need to Succeed

This cheerfully designed publication was compiled to highlight what we know about risk factors as well as strategies for supporting each child's emerging competence.

Available online at http://www.casel.org/downloads/goodbeginning.pdf

The Impact of Inclusion on Language Development and Social Competence Among Preschoolers With Disabilities
Y. Rafferty, V. Piscitelli, & C. Boettche

Inclusion is not a guarantor of academic success. This article cites recent research showing that program quality and the availability of support services are essential to the social-emotional and cognitive competence of all children in inclusive settings.

Available online at http://journals.sped.org/EC/Archive_Articles/
VOLUME69NUMBER4Summer2003_EC_Article-5.pdf

Promoting the Emotional Well-Being of Children and Families. Policy Paper No. 3: Ready To Enter: What Research Tells Policymakers About Strategies to Promote Social and Emotional School Readiness Among Three- and Four-Year-Old Children
Mailman School of Public Health, National Center for Children in Poverty (Columbia University)

Issue briefs synthesize recent research that shows the relationship of social and emotional well-being to school achievement. Written primarily for policymakers and program administrators, these briefs address fiscal and policy-level challenges they may encounter as they try to provide the resources that young children need for healthy growth and development.

Available online at http://www.nccp.org/media/pew02c-text.pdf

Set for Success: Building a Strong Foundation for School Readiness Based on the Social-Emotional Development of Young Children

Kaufmann Early Education Exchange, 2002 Conference Series Report (Kaufmann Foundation Fulfillment Center)

This Ewing Marion Kauffman Foundation report compiled seven papers that present the latest scientific findings on the importance of social and emotional school readiness as a precursor to cognitive competence. The papers also provide compelling evidence of programs that help to prepare young children for early school success.

Available online at http://www.kauffman.org/pdf/eex_brochure.pdf (121-page document) and http://www.kauffman.org/pdf/eex_summary.pdf (executive summary)

Social-Emotional Learning in Early Childhood: What We Know and Where to Go from Here

S. A. Denham & R. P. Weissberg

Partnerships of schools, families, and communities provide the context for learning about human relationships. The authors call for more focused attention on classroom practices that enhance social and emotional learning throughout the childhood and teenage years.

Available online at http://www.casel.org/downloads/SELearlychildhood.pdf

Strengthening Social and Emotional Competence in Young Children–The Foundation for Early School Readiness and Success

C. Webster-Stratton & M. J. Reid

The Incredible Years Dinosaur Social Skills and Problem-Solving Child Training Program teaches social skills to young children with the confidence that social competence is strongly related to school readiness and academic success. In the Dinosaur program, children learn anger management and problem-solving techniques; they learn to understand and recognize feelings; and, they practice communicating and being friendly with others.

Available online at http://www.son.washington.edu/centers/parenting-clinic/opendocs/strengthening2004.pdf

The Teaching Pyramid: A Model for Supporting Social Competence and Preventing Challenging Behavior in Young Children

L. Fox, G. Dunlap, M. L. Hemmeter, G. E. Joseph, & P. S. Strain

With the teaching pyramid, early childhood professionals support social competence by building on a foundation of positive relationships at school and at home, designing classroom environments that elicit pro-social behaviors, and implementing social and emotional teaching strategies. The most intensive level of support at the top of the pyramid is individualized intervention based on assessments by professionals and family members.

Available online at http://challengingbehavior.fmhi.usf.edu/handouts/yc_article.pdf

Using Culturally Responsive Activities to Promote Social Competence and Classroom Community
W. A. Harriott & S. S. Martin

As teachers face the challenges of addressing diversity and supporting social acceptance, it becomes crucial to create supportive classroom communities. This article offers sample activities and resources to support social competence and communication.

Available online at: http://journals.sped.org/EC/Archive_Articles/
VOL.37NO.1SeptOct2004_TEC_Harriott37-1.pdf